From Boiling Water
the Southern European Cuisine

A TRAVELOGUE

From Boiling Water to Master of the Southern European Cuisine

A TRAVELOGUE

Copyright © 2023 by Janisa J. Brunstein

All rights reserved.
No part of this publication may be reproduced in any form, by photostat, microfilm, xerography, or any other means, or incorporated into any information retrieval system, electronic or mechanical, without the written permission of the copyright writer.

All inquiries should be addressed to:

Book Savvy International Inc.
1626 Clear View Drive, Beverly Hills California 90210, United States

Hotline: (213) 855-4299
https://booksavvyinternationalinc.com/

Ordering Information:
Bulk orders, pricing inquiries and special rebates are accessible on the amount bought by corporations, associations, and others. For points of interest, contact the distributor at the address above.

Printed in the United States of America.

ISBN-13	Hardback	979-8-89190-123-0
	Paperback	979-8-89190-122-3
	eBook	979-8-89190-121-6

Library of Congress Control Number: 2023923134

Dedication

I do not have enough words to appreciate everything my husband has done for me; he is my friend, my pivotal rock, and my companion, but most of all, he is so special. He is the one who has been taking me on all these adventures around the world; without him, it would not have been possible for me to write this book. And now, I'm able to narrate it to all the readers and to all those interested in adventures and good cuisine.

To my parents, for their unconditional support and for being there when I needed it, whether in the good times or not so much. With their education and dedication, they have been teaching me since I was a little girl what perseverance, responsibility, and constancy are; otherwise, I could not have finished this book.

To my beautiful sons and grandkids, who are my dream and inspiration in my life. They are the impulse for me to continue; it's my gift to them to leave them a good legacy and memoirs.

And for the readers, to whom I believe this book will bring joy and excitement and create a thirst for adventure, to start strolling the world. It will create a new perspective on life. The world gives plenty of knowledge that is very difficult to gather from school or from all my family and friends, from whom I have, in one way or another, been learning.

And finally, to all those I don't remember this time, from the bottom of my heart, I say thank you.

Janisa Brunstein.

Contents

CHAPTER I:

Shuffling Off To Buffalo 1

CHAPTER II:

A Trip to Buffalo 4

CHAPTER III 7

CHAPTER IV:

The Christmas Gala Fiasco 8

CHRISTMAS GALA PHOTOS 10

CHRISTMAS GALA RECIPES 21

Mini Lime Pies 22

Thai Crabmeat Spring Rolls 23

Christmas Gala Dessert 25

Strawberry Shortcake 26

CHAPTER V:

Dinner For My Valentine 30

VALENTINE DINNER RECIPES 36

Pomegranate Honey Roasted Chicken 37

Quinoa Cake with Cajun & Vegetables. 39

Sweet Potato Tzimmes with Apricot & Apple Sauce. 40

Turkey Meatloaf with Mushrooms 42

Valentine Dessert. 43

Chocolate and Chocolate Fudge 44

Dark Chocolate Cake with Strawberries 45

Rose Petal Frosting 45

Gluten Free & Dairy Free Banana Bread with Walnuts. 46

CHEESECAKE 47

GLUTEN & DAIRY FREE CARROT CAKE WITH WALNUTS 48

VANILLA POUND CAKE 49

CHOCOLATE CAKE WITH KIRSCH 49

PLUM DAIRY FREE CAKE 52

CHAPTER VI:

A Trip to Italy. 54

Italy Photos 60

Italian Gnocchi With Marinara Sauce Only 61

Mandamento Palazzo Market, Palermo, Sicily. 62

Market Vegetable Stand, Palermo, Sicily 63

Castellammare del Golfo, Sicily 64

Custonaci, Sicily 65

On the street in Trapani, Sicily 66

Trapani, Sicily 67

San Vito lo Capo, Italy 68

ITALIAN RECIPES 69

Asparagus Risotto 70

Baked Eggplant Parmesan 71

Caesar Salad 72

Chicken Marsala with Mushrooms 73

Eggplant Rollatini 74

Fettuccine with Tomato Sauce, Cauliflower & Anchovies .76

Linguine with Shrimp & Scallops 78

JANISA'S HOMEMADEN NEPOLITARIAN MARINARA SAUCE 79

JANISA'S PERFECT NEPOLITANIAN PIZZA 80

FOR THE MARINARA SAUCE 80

Pan Fried Fillet of Sole with Lemon Butter Sauce in a Polenta Bed 81

Pasta Dough for Ravioli 83

Pumpkin Ravioli with Tomatoes & Ricotta 85

Truffle Risotto 86

Other Recipe 87

ITALIAN DESSERT 89

Italian Blueberry Polenta Dessert 90

Italian Profiteroles Dessert 92

CHAPTER VII:

A Trip To Spain 93

Madrid, Spain 98

BARCELONA PHOTOS 103

Basilica De la Sagrada Familia 105

Architecture of Barcelona 106

A Trip to La Coruña 109

Palma de Mallorca, Spain 116

Cathedral Santa Maria de Mallorca Palma de Mallorca, Spain 117

Aerial Views: Palma de Mallorca Coast, Spain 117

Cala Major Palma 118

Palacio de la Almudeina Interior View 118

Soller, Palma de Mallorca 119

Palma de Mallorca, Spain 120

Palma de Mallorca, Spain 121

Palma de Mallorca, Spain 123

Palma de Mallorca, Spain 124

Palma de Mallorca, Spain 125

SPANISH RECIPES 126

Andalusian Gazpacho 127

Breaded Baked Tomatoes 128

Chilled Almond & Garlic Soup 129

Cold Watermelon Salad 130

Crema Catalana (Catalan Custard). 131

Ensalada Mixta (Mixed Salad) 132

Ensalada de Frutas (Fruit Salad) 133

Grilled Eggplant & Red Peppers 134

Grouper in Matelote Sauce. 135

Seafood Paella 136

Tortillas de Patatas (Potato Omelet) 138

CHAPTER VIII:

A Trip to France. 139

Paris Skyline 146

Storefront Desserts, Paris 147

French Recipes 148

Caramelized Onion Tart 149

Omelette Quercynoise 151

French Pumpkin Soup 152

French Carrot Salad with Lemon Dijon 153

Endive Red Apple Salad 154

Carbonnade Belgium Beef & Beer Stew 155

Pommel De Terre Au Gratin (Potato Gratin) 156

Papeton D'Aubergines (Molded Eggplant Pudding) .157

Anchoiade Anchovy Spread 159

Cervelle De Canut (Herbed Cheese Spread) 160

French Dessert 161

Gâteau Basque (Basque Cake) 162

Grenoblois (Grenoble Caramel Walnut Cake) 164

FRENCH SWEET CREPES WITH STRABERRY SAUCE (DAIRY FREE OPTION)...165

STRABERRY SAUCE 166

CHAPTER IX:

A Trip to Portugal 167

Photo Sant George Castle. Lisbon, Portugal 169

CHAPTER X:

A Trip To Greece (Crete) 174

Greece Photos 177

At Hotel Entrance in Crete 178

Analipsi & Sitia, Lasithi, Greece 179

Makrygialos, Greece 180

Heraklion Port, Greece 182

Aghios Nikolaos Bay, Greece 183

GREEK RECIPES 184

Greek Appetizers 185

Spanakopita (Spinach Phyllo Pie) 185

Chickpea Rissoles 187

Greek Hummus 188

Shrimp-Filled Phyllo Rolls 189

Little Herbed Meatballs 190

Retsina-Pickled Octopus or Squid 191

Greek Side Dishes 193

Greek Olive Bread 194

Braised Artichokes with Fresh Peas 195

Greek Potato Zucchini Casserole 197

Greek Tomato and Potato Bake 198

Russian Salad 199

Greek Dessert 200

Baklava 201

Date & Almond Tart 203

CHAPTER XI:

Back in the Train to Buffalo 205

CHAPTER I

INTRODUCTION:

Shuffling Off To Buffalo

It was a scorching hot day, one of the last days of the summer of 2016. I was at the entrance of the Croton Harmon train station in Westchester County, New York, preparing to travel to Buffalo to meet my granddaughter Lily for the first time. My husband told me to enjoy my time with Lily, gave me a hug, kiss, and a warm goodbye, and left.

I managed to pull my small but heavy suitcase up the stairs to the second floor to get information about my train ride. An official there gave me detailed instructions: I should take an elevator down to Track 1 and wait by the left side, because only certain train doors would open, and that was the side where the conductor would be requesting tickets. I thought to myself this was no time to be lazy, so I skipped the elevator and trudged down to Track 1.

There I was, in front of a big, round clock, a green garbage basket, and a square electronic sign showing arrivals, departures, and destinations. I saw a black lady sitting in a wooden chair and a middle-aged man standing. He resembled an artist who'd been burned in a fire. I wanted to talk—in those days, I needed to clear out the debris cluttering my brain. I called this my Delusion Reality. I approached the man and asked if he was an artist. He seemed confused and excited, and responded in his taciturn voice, "I'm flattered, but I'm actually a bank teller." Somehow, I didn't believe him.

I had dressed accordingly for the heat, in a blue short skirt and a blue cotton sleeveless dressy shirt, but I was still sweating as I waited for the train and daydreamed of being in comfy air conditioning. I hoped there would be no train delays.

A few minutes after 11:15, the train pulled into the station. Luckily, I was already in line, and the conductor directed me to sit on the left aisle of the coach section. People were packed in like sardines on that Labor Day weekend. Nearly every seat was occupied; my choices were limited. I could sit in an aisle seat next to a heavy-set woman with no room to move. There was a seat on the end train car near the restroom—no toilet odors for me! My only other option was another aisle seat, which had its tabletop down to hold a laptop for its owner: a handsome young man seated by a window. I wandered aimlessly down the aisles, until the man offered to remove his computer and let me have that seat. I gratefully accepted, and I slung my mini suitcase into the upper compartment, put my handbag on the floor, and settled in.

Discreetly, out of the corner of my eye, I glanced at my seat companion. He was listening to music on his phone and working on a spreadsheet on his computer, which filled with columns and rows of large number amounts. After the train departed, I soaked up the amazing, natural New York scenery and felt inspired. I looked at the young man and he smiled at me. I opened my iPad and continued reading a book I'd started about G-d. Lately I'd become very interested in learning about and feeling more connected to our creator. At the age of 47, I'd developed a thirst for knowledge. On my night table at home, I had a pile of books I read with enthusiasm, and before I went to bed, I liked to improve my sketching by drawing from the Maestros in my sketchbook. Recently, I'd gone to a painting class at my synagogue, and I enjoyed it so much that the next day I bought a painting kit at the art store and discovered another talent. When I painted, I was totally present in the moment, and it was an antidote for my anxiety and a cure for my mood swings. I listened to classical music (especially Mozart) while I painted, which opened up another amazing world of colors and imagination. I believe that until we try new things, we don't know what kind of wood we're made of. Now I know.

Inside the train, I spotted a woman who reminded me of another I saw at a special Christmas party I'd attended with my former husband. I will describe this in the next chapter.

My seatmate continued working on his computer. Suddenly, he got a phone call and started to dictate big numbers to the person on the other end: $2 million in New York City, $3 million in Toronto, many more millions around the country. I realized he was reporting his sales figures. It was a long conversation (about thirty minutes), and listening to it was raising my adrenaline, but I tried to keep my composure and be patient and respectful. When he finished, I expressed my astonishment about the figures he'd mentioned. He replied that he was a salesperson and was giving his boss month-end sales totals. I thought to myself that he probably earned good money—but then I noticed he wore a wedding band. We continued our conversation. I learned he was a graduate of West Point (one of the world's most recognized army academies) and was a retired army official and police sheriff at Stewart Airport in Newburgh, New York. He'd met his wife in the army twenty-five years ago; they had five grown children (one married) and one granddaughter. He showed me photos of his typical American family—kids, house, car, jobs, and sports. I thought to myself, Some of these are the bread of life, and others (like sports and amusements) are the circus, a way of escaping the pressures and problems of society and applying entropy—energy for the non-essential but joyous aspects of life.

He asked me my nationality. I smiled and answered proudly that I was a Venezuelan Jewish girl and also a polyglot, which probably made my accent hard to decipher.

Now I decided it was time to recount my adventures in traveling, cooking, and culture in Southern Europe. So, my journey begins, as told to my captive companion on the train to Buffalo…

CHAPTER II

A Trip to Buffalo

He left me at the entrance of Croton - Harmon train station in Westchester County, NY, giving me a hug and a kiss, telling me to enjoy Lily, who I went to meet for my first time, and then a warm goodbye was his final word.

I took my small suitcase and rolled to the stairs, managing to pull it up. I needed to find information, and when I reached the second floor, I found an official and asked him for the train track to Buffalo. He told me the way. He also realized how heavy my luggage was, so he advised me to take the elevator down to Track 1.

I thought, I can't be lazy, and deciding to exercise myself, I lifted my suitcase and walked down the stairs to Track 1.

A few minutes later, I was there in front the track. I walked to the left side, because the official had advised me in advance that on this train, only certain doors opened, and the conductor would appear on this side requesting the tickets.

There I was in front of a big round clock and a square electronic sign showing arrivals, departures, and destinations. Nearby, a lady of color sat in a wooden chair, and a middle-aged man was standing. He looked like an artist who'd been burned in a fire.

I wanted to talk; it was my outlet in those days when I strongly need to get rid of the garbage I had been keeping in my brain. I call it my Delusion Reality. So, I approached the man and asked if he was an artist, just to make conversation, and he responded in his taciturn voice, shifting between excitement and confusion, "I'm flattered." But he added that he was a bank teller. From his voice of disbelief, I immediately thought he was lying.

It was a hot day, one of the last of the summer of 2016, with no breeze to refresh me. Even though I had dressed accordingly, as I usually did, with a blue short skirt and a blue cotton sleeveless dressy shirt, I was sweating while waiting for the train. I was hoping for no train delays and daydreaming about comfy AC.

Suddenly, a few minutes after 11:15 a.m., the train reached the station, the door opened, and the conductor came out from one of the left doors and started requesting tickets. I was already in line and the conductor asked for my name. After giving it, he looked at his list and knew who I was and where to place me. He told me to go to the left car of the train.

Once inside, I realized how packed and crowded the train was. Besides my decision to travel on a Thursday, it was also a long Labor Day weekend approaching the autumn of 2016.

I walked down the aisle and glanced at all the rows, with two seats to the right and two seats to the left, but all of them were occupied. Only a couple seats were available, one of which was an aisle seat next to a heavy lady, in which the little space left for me didn't appear to my liking. Another seat was available by the aisle in the opposite direction, but the coffee table was down and on top was a computer that belonged to a young man seated by the window.

Further down, a few other seats near the end of the train car by the restroom were available, but I would never pick one of them because of the odors that would start to emanate after several usages. I knew this from previous trips when I had been seated next to the toilets.

There were no other options, unless one counted the cafeteria, which had a few lunch tables, about three of them on each side of the train car.

After I walked back and forth through the car, the young man with the computer and the smart phone turned to me and made a hand motion, asking if I wanted to sit there by the aisle.

I responded affirmatively and he moved the computer and closed the coffee table so I could sit. I lifted my mini suitcase to the upper compartment, put my handbag on the floor, and sat.

The young man continued working. Out of the corner of my eyes, I saw that he was working on a spreadsheet, its columns and rows filled with big numbers. While he listened to music, I looked around, getting familiar with my surroundings.

The train soon took off.

CHAPTER III

After taking off, I kept looking outside, inspired by the terrific natural scenery of amazing NY state.

I looked at the young man and he smiled at me. Then I took my iPad and continued reading my book about G-d. I had been very interested in that matter, in getting to know and be more connected with the creator. At my age, I had discovered I wanted to learn more. Everything had become a subject of interest. On my night table at home, I had a pile of books on different subjects, which I read with enthusiasm. I also had a sketchbook, in which I tried to draw from the Maestros every night before going to bed so I could improve.

I went to a painting class near my synagogue that I enjoyed so much that the next day, I went to an art store and bought a painting start kit. I'd discovered another talent.

When I paint, for me, it's like being totally present in that very moment. It's a medicine to my anxieties, a cure for my swing moods. When I paint, I play classic music, especially Mozart, and there, I focus on another amazing world of colors and imagination.

Inside the train, I saw a lady who reminded me of a special Christmas party I'd attended with my former husband.

CHAPTER IV

The Christmas Gala Fiasco

My then-husband and I were sponsoring a special gala Christmas party as a fundraiser. I planned all the menus and recipes for the cooks. The day of the gala, I awoke early and started my day like any other. First, I stepped on the treadmill for exercise, then my yoga instructor came and I did yoga for one hour in my private gym. The housekeeper prepared a healthy breakfast for me—homemade cappuccino with whipped cream and chocolate powder on top, fruit salad, oatmeal, fresh-squeezed orange juice, and Greek yogurt with a homemade granola mix I'd created, made with dried seeds, coconut flakes, and raisins.

In the morning, my mind is very clear and creative, so during breakfast, I answered some emails, took notes, and grabbed the daily newspaper the housekeeper always put on the table. Before leaving for work, my husband excitedly checked a newspaper article that mentioned our donation to the city library. After breakfast, I did more work on the computer, took a shower, got dressed, and had our chauffeur drive me to the beauty parlor to have my hair done for the party.

Although I felt energetic, I was mentally burdened by a feeling of jealousy. My intuition told me my husband was having an affair with a coworker. I knew it just by looking at him and seeing the changes in his appearance and behavior. All the signs were there: he had lost weight. He paid more attention to every detail of his appearance. I knew he gave gifts to this stranger. Of course, he denied all of this, and I acted like it wasn't happening, but it was an open secret.

Later, our chauffeur dropped us off in the valet parking area at the entrance of the party, where we were welcomed by our friendly, smiling host, who collected our invitations. We were escorted through a long aisle in a room with an opulent crystal chandelier on the ceiling, up to the ballroom on the second floor. The décor and ambiance were impressively upscale and elegant. There were small white Christmas lights everywhere, and a huge Christmas tree with lots of gifts under it. Tables were covered purple and gold tablecloths, as well as mixtures of short and tall tropical and Asian flower bouquets. The tables were around the dance floor, in front of the orchestra. There was also a table of appetizers: hors d'oeuvres, imported cheeses, and charcuterie (cold cuts), as well as a bar, and a tower built with champagne glasses. There was even a room for canine guests near the service door!

At the party, I started ruminating about what was going on between my husband and me, and I arrived at an absurd and inappropriate idea of how to boost my self-esteem: I would change my hair color, right there at the party! When I get an idea, I feel compelled to make it a reality—I really have to be careful what I'm thinking! So, in the middle of the orchestra performance, like a full-fledged maniac filled with determination, I left the party. I had my driver take me to a nearby beauty store. I asked the hair expert there what type of tools and dye I needed to dye my hair myself. She advised me to get bleach powder, peroxide, a bowl, and a brush that looked like a bakery brush—I would know this, because on top of everything else, I'm an executive chef. I was usually the one who cooked and prepared menus for all types of gatherings. I bought everything the beautician recommended and headed back to the party.

I managed to unobtrusively enter the kitchen and mix up the chemical concoction for my hair. I thought I'd added too much water, but I couldn't add more powder. So, with the mixture slithering down my head, with great nervousness and embarrassment, I walked back to our table.

Believe it or not, there was a dog food station for the guests' dogs, where the dogs had an awesome array of sophisticated treats of various sizes and shapes in bowls. It smelled like you were at an Oktoberfest festival, next to the hot dog trucks! The dogs also had a mobile dog gym, a mobile nail salon/grooming station, professional dog sitters, and even doggie beds for the ones that got exhausted. I thought perhaps one of the groomers could up-do my hair after I was done with the color.

Lo and behold, while walking to our table, some of the mixture spilled off my head, straight into the dogs' serving station. I quickly tried to clean up the mess by dropping the dog food into the nearest water drain. To my horror, the drain became clogged and water started backing up like Niagara Falls in reverse, spewing dirty sewer water over all the party floor! You couldn't imagine the chaos that ensued: women started lifting their long, beautiful, expensive gowns and screaming like banshees, trying to keep their manners while emptying the place as quickly as possible. They bumped into each other and into waiters passing out the final hors d'oeuvres, and some fell on the floor like wild horses who didn't want anyone to ride them. Some people tried to reach their dogs; others couldn't even recognize their dogs in the mêlée.

That was how the party ended.

Reception Area

Entrance to Reception Area

Party Christmas Tree

Bar Area

Passing Pastries

CHRISTMAS GALA RECIPES

Mini Lime Pies

Crust:
1 ½ cups graham or coffee crackers
4 Tbsp. light corn syrup
5 Tbsp. melted butter

Filling:
2/3 cup heavy cream
Grated lime zest
4 Tbsp. fresh-squeezed juice (2 limes)
7 oz. canned sweetened condensed milk
Extra lime zest (garnish)

Directions:

Preheat oven to 350°F. Lightly grease two 12-section mini muffin pans. Put butter and syrup in a saucepan and heat while gently uncovered, until butter melts. Remove from heat and stir in cracker crumbs. Divide mixture among the prepared pans. Press mixture firmly over the bottom and side of pans with the back of a spoon. Bake for 6 minutes or until dark golden brown. Let cool for about 15 minutes.

Meanwhile, pour cream in a bowl, add lime zest, and whisk until thickened. Gradually whisk the condensed milk, add lime juice, and whisk for another few minutes until the mixture has thickened. Use a round blade knife to carefully lift pies from the pans. Pipe or spoon lime cream into the pie shells. Chill for at least 30 minutes. Garnish with lime zest.

Thai Crabmeat Spring Rolls

12 oz. jumbo crabmeat
2 egg whites
4 Tbsp. scallions
2 Tsp. lime juice
24 wonton wrappers
1 cup vegetable oil
Cilantro (garnish)
2 Tbsp. sesame seeds, toasted.
1 Tbsp. ginger peeled and grated.
1 Tbsp. soy sauce
½ Tsp. kosher salt
Water
1 Tbsp. cornstarch for dusting

Dipping Sauce:
½ Tsp. coriander seeds
1 dried Thai red chili
1 ½ Tbsp. brown sugar
½ Tsp. sesame oil
1 Tbsp. sake
1 ½ Tsp. star anise pods
½ cup water
1" lemongrass, crushed.
3 Tbsp. soy sauce

Directions:

To prepare spring rolls/filling: Mix all ingredients for filling and set aside. Place about 1 ½ tbsp. of crabmeat mixture in a narrow strip along the side of a rectangular baking sheet and spread out the full length. Roll wonton wrapper once over the mixture. Continue rolling until the filled wrapper is in a one long roll. Starting at one end of the roll, turn the roll into itself, continuing round and round to make a coil. Place the coil on the prepared baking sheet, seam side down. Dust with cornstarch.

To cook spring rolls: in a large skillet, heat oil over medium heat until hot, but not smoking. Fry spring rolls until golden. Serve immediately with dipping sauce.

Dipping sauce: In a small saucepan, toast coriander seeds with anise and red chili. Add water, sugar, and lemongrass and bring to a boil. Let simmer for 5-10 minutes. Stir in sesame oil, soy sauce, and sake. Transfer to a serving bowl. Garnish with cilantro.

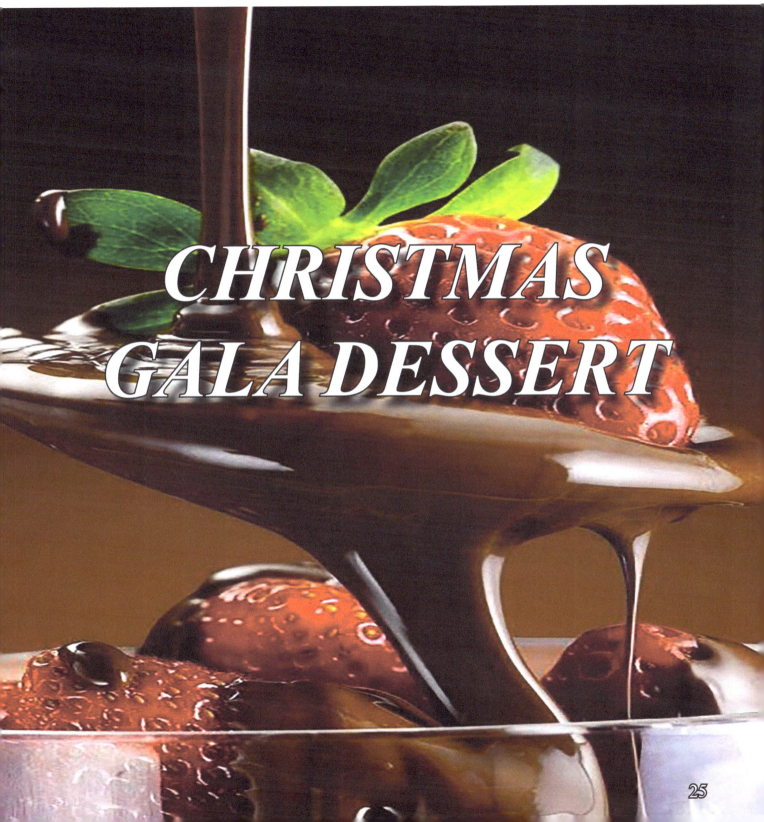

Strawberry Shortcake

2 sticks (16 Tbsp.) butter
6 eggs
1 cup milk
Pinch of salt
Strawberries (garnish)

2 ½ cups sugar
2 ¾ cups all-purpose flour
½ Tbsp. baking powder
whipping cream (topping)

Filling:
1 cup milk
1/3 cup powdered sugar
1 Tbsp. dark rum

3 egg yolks
¼ cup all-purpose flour
1 Tsp. vanilla

Directions:

Use eggbeater to beat butter and sugar until they form cream. Pour in eggs and continue beating for about 8 minutes. Add flour, milk, and vanilla extract. Prepare a round 11" x 3" cake pan with wax paper. Pour the mixture and bake at 350°F for about 45 minutes, or until you prick a toothpick in the center of the cake and it comes clean. Remove from oven and let cool completely. Divide the cake into 3 equal parts.

Meanwhile, prepare the filling. Bring milk to simmer in a small saucepan. Combine egg yolks and sugar in a large saucepan and whisk until pale in color. Mix in flour and pour in hot milk. Place saucepan over low heat and cook custard until it thickens, beating constantly. Let boil for 1 minute, then remove from heat. Add rum and vanilla. Let cool, stirring occasionally.

Spread filling in each part of the cake. Spread whipping cream on top and garnish with strawberries.

CHAPTER V

Dinner For My Valentine

One Valentine's Day, I planned a special menu for an exotic gourmet dinner to impress my lover, and I set the scene for love, passion, and seduction. Each dish had ingredients that were sensuous and had aphrodisiac properties, including chocolate, rose petals, chilies, and red wine.

The day before, I grabbed my shopping list and headed to our community farmer's market to buy the ingredients. I noticed the floor there was covered in gravel, and it was a challenge to walk in my high heels. One gentleman stared at me and flirtatiously commented that he liked my shoes, and that my lipstick matched my outfit. I smiled at him and made my way through the vegetable stands. I'd been a loyal customer for years, so some stand owners greeted me with a warm welcome. When I walked, I swung my hips in a sexy way, as if I were dancing a samba. I liked to think that when I looked young and attractive, people could feel the beauty in my soul, and that it was like therapy for them.

I spent lots of time picking chilies of various colors and textures: red, green, yellow, tiny but hot, big with a chocolate scent. Even though I could tell the different aromas by heart, I discreetly sniffed the chilies several times to make sure they were very fresh, colorful, and rich in flavor. I also bought cilantro, vanilla, garlic, onions, and spices. A gentleman helped me put everything in my car.

On the evening of Valentine's Day, I started cooking. It was a cold, windy day. I put my apron on and focused my energy on my fabulous dishes. I took out my pans, saucepans, and skillet to sauté what was needed—I firmly believed everything in the kitchen started with sautéed garlic and onions. In a heavy skillet, I sautéed garlic and onions until they were brownish, then added the chilies. I was in heaven: the smells in my kitchen transported me on a trip to goodness. To me, it was not a job, but a total pleasure, doing what I loved. I danced to music on my stereo in the kitchen—bossa nova, salsa, classical music like Turangalila—and the symphonic sounds inspired me and put me in the mood. The love and good vibrations permeated every corner of my house. After sautéing the chilies, I added them to my boiling Cornish hen broth. I had previously marinated my glatt kosher duck in French spices, anise, and cherry liqueur; after braising it, I placed it in the oven to roast for about two hours. Duck meat is always hard and needs lots of cooking time.

In the meantime, I set and decorated the dining table in a formal, royal style. First, I laid a cushiony cloth along the table with a long, white linen tablecloth on top and a large, black and white polka-dotted runner in the middle. I set two red satin rectangular placemats for each of us. I selected my Clarissa Cliff English hand-painted china and my just-polished 100% silverware: first a large black rectangular plate, then a medium black rectangular plate for the main course, then a round black soup bowl on top. On the right, I placed the knife facing the plates, the soup spoon, and authentic Czech rose crystal glasses with a gold rim, one for red wine and another for water. In front of the dishes, I placed a dessert spoon facing up.

I'd ordered four dozen Dutch satin red roses and foliage for the centerpieces. I set them in three arrangements: one large crystal jar with two dozen tall roses and foliage, and two smaller centerpieces with six small roses each on each side of the runner. In between the centerpieces, I placed two small round mirrors, each with a silver candelabra and a long white candle.

My deck was near my neighbor's window. She knocked on my door and asked me what delicious, glorious food I was cooking, because she could smell it! When I described my special menu planned for the evening, she was very impressed with my talents.

When I finished my cooking, I put everything in silver trays, saucers, and bowls, so it would be ready to serve. Now it was time for me to get myself ready. I took a bath. I wanted my skin to look radiant and glowing, so I treated myself to Dead Sea salts, coconut foaming bubbles, and an antioxidant enzyme face scrub. For a final touch, I moisturized my skin with mineral butter. For my wardrobe, I chose black and red French Belford lingerie (which I'd bought a year before when I'd gone for my cooking shows in Paris), and a knee-length, sleeveless, beaded dress of navy blue, army green, and orange, with gold embroidery. I did a French twist up-do for my hair. For makeup, I wore smoky eyeliner and eyeshadow, orange lipstick that matched my dress, and army green nail polish, with a gold ring on my finger.

At 7:05, my doorbell rang. I got excited, and for one second, I imagined everything that would happen that night: amazing food, beautiful company, and lots and lots of love. I opened the door and there he was, meticulously groomed, wearing a rich, seductive cologne and neatly pressed clothes, like he was ready for his army graduation! He kissed my cheek and gave me a bouquet of flowers he'd been hiding behind his back. He asked if I needed any help, but everything was ready to be served. I poured the champagne and we sat down and started our festivities. It was all worth it—I was with the man I wanted, celebrating Valentine's Day in style!

VALENTINE DINNER RECIPES

Pomegranate Honey Roasted Chicken

1 whole chicken with skin
½ cup honey
¼ cup brown sugar
¼ cup pomegranate juice
¼ cup teriyaki sauce
4 Tbsp. tomato paste

½ Tbsp. fresh thyme
2 fresh garlic cloves
1 Tbsp. butter
1 Tbsp. olive oil
Pomegranate seeds (garnish)

Directions:

Arrange chicken in a baking dish and set aside. In a saucepan, pour in olive oil and melt butter over medium heat. Add garlic and onion and sauté them until brownish. Add brown sugar and let it melt, stirring constantly. Add pomegranate juice, teriyaki sauce, tomato paste, and thyme, and stir. Bring to a simmer for about 5 minutes. Generously brush chicken with the mixture and marinate overnight.

Preheat oven to 350°F. Cover chicken with aluminum foil and bake until chicken reaches an inside temperature of 160°F; it should be brown and crispy outside. Transfer to a serving plate and baste again with the juices., Garnish with pomegranate seeds and thyme leaves. Serve immediately.

Quinoa Cake With Cajun & Vegetables

- 1 cup red quinoa
- 1 cup regular quinoa
- 4 cups chicken or vegetable stock
- 1 bunch of scallions, thinly sliced
- 2 eggs, beaten
- ½ cup breadcrumbs
- 1 small diced red onion
- 1 jalapeño pepper
- 2 cloves garlic
- 2 plum tomatoes
- 1 Tbsp. olive oil
- 1 Tsp. fresh thyme
- 1 Tbsp. of Cajun spice
- Pepper to taste
- Alfalfa (garnish)
- Cherry tomatoes (garnish)

Directions:

Mix red and regular quinoa. Rinse in a mesh strainer to remove the starch coat. In a pan, cook quinoa with chicken or vegetable stock over low flame, until stock evaporates completely and quinoa is cooked. Set aside to cool. In a skillet, sauté garlic and red onion until clear. Add jalapeño, tomatoes, scallions, thyme, Cajun spice, and pepper. After quinoa is cool, mix with sautéed vegetables, eggs, and breadcrumbs. Transfer mixture to a coffee pan and bake at 350°F for 45-50 minutes. When cool, transfer to a serving platter; garnish and decorate with alfalfa and cherry tomatoes.

Sweet Potato Tzimmes with Apricot & Apple Sauce

1 large red-skinned yam (sweet potato), about 1 ½ lbs.
1 ¼ Tsp. ground ginger
1/3 Tbsp. apricot jam
5 large eggs
3 cups apple juice
1 ¼ cups matzo meal
16 oz. pkg. dried apricots
1 ½ sticks (12 Tbsp.) unsalted butter
1 cinnamon stick
1 ½ Tbsp. sugar
Chopped mint (garnish)
1 3/4 Tbsp. salt

Directions:

Cut potatoes in half and pierce with fork. Wrap in aluminum foil and bake at 350°F for 45 minutes or until tender inside. Scoop out 1 ¼ cups of potatoes, let cool, and mix with matzo meal, eggs, 2 tbsp. of butter, sugar, salt, and ginger until blended. Transfer to a bowl. Cover and chill overnight until firm. Using wet hands, roll mixture into balls. Cook potato balls in salted boiling water until they're tender and float to the top. Using a slotted spoon, transfer to plate or sheet of aluminum foil. Repeat with the remaining mixture. Let stand firm, at least 30 minutes. Melt 5 ½ tbsp. of butter in a heavy skillet over medium-high heat. Add the balls and sauté them until brown, about 5 minutes. Transfer to a 13" x 9" x 2" glass baking dish.

Sauce: Bring jam and apricots to boil in a small saucepan. Cover until apricots are tender, about 10 minutes. Drain juices into a medium saucepan and add cinnamon. Add the remaining butter and jam. Simmer over medium heat until reduced to ¾ cup, about 15 minutes. Return apricots to sauce. Add balls to sauce. Let cool, garnish with chopped mint, and serve.

Turkey Meatloaf with Mushrooms

2 Tbsp. olive oil
2 cups French baguette flour
8 oz. mushrooms, sliced
2 large eggs, beaten
¼ cup shallots, chopped
2 Tbsp. parsley leaves, chopped
1 Tbsp. fresh thyme
2 lbs. ground turkey
1 beef cube
Salt and pepper to taste

Directions:

Soak bread in water. In a medium skillet, at medium-high heat, sauté the shallots until brown. Add mushrooms and parsley and cook for about 6 minutes. Add the beef cube and wait until it's totally melted. Add salt and pepper to taste. In a bowl, add eggs, squeeze dry bread, turkey, and vegetables, and stir until fully mixed. Prepare a cake pan with parchment paper; pour in the meat mixture. Bake at 350°F for 35-40 minutes or until golden brown. Serve hot.

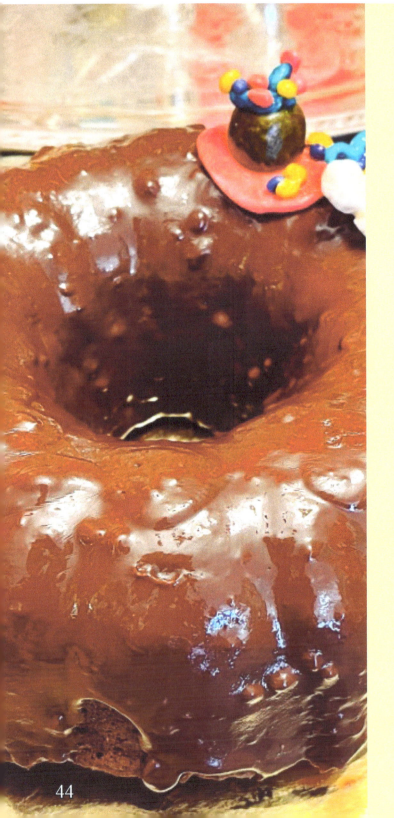

Chocolate And Chocolate Fudge

180 gm of All-purpose flour
280 gm of sugar
120 ml of canola oil or sunflower oil
160 ml of milk
100 ml of boiling water
2 eggs
60 gm unsweetened cocoa
1 Tbsp. vanilla
Pinch of salt
2 Tbsp. of baking powder

Directions:

Beat the eggs in the mixer at high speed for 5 minutes, until the eggs whiten. Then add the sugar and beat for one more minute. Add the smooth canola oil, milk, and vanilla extract. In a separate bowl, sift the flour with cocoa and baking powder.

After the dry ingredients are sifted, add the salt to boost the flavor of the cake. Finally, add the liquid mixture to it with the mixer off. Just fold the ingredients and then turn on the mixer at a slow speed. When the mixture is all incorporated, add the boiling water. Prepare the mold in a 18cm x 10 cm pan with wax paper and pour the cake mixture into. Put it in a preheated oven. Bake at 350°F for about 50 minutes.

Dark Chocolate Cake with Strawberries

Rose Petal Frosting

2 eggs
1 Tbsp. vanilla extract
Pinch of salt
½ cup unsweetened cocoa

½ cup canola or sunflower oil
2/3 cup milk
2 Tbsp. baking powder
Fudge

1 ½ cups sugar
1 ½ cups all-purpose flour
Strawberries
½ cup boiling water

Directions:

Beat eggs in mixer at high speed for 5 minutes, until eggs whiten. Add sugar and beat for one more minute. Add canola or sunflower oil, milk, and vanilla extract. In a separate bowl, sift flour with cocoa and baking powder. Add salt to boost the cake's flavor. Add the liquid mixture to the ingredients in the bowl, just folding the ingredients. Use mixer at slow speed. When fully mixed, add boiling water. Preheat oven to 350°F. In a cake mold, use baking spray or 7" x 4" wax paper. Pour the cake mixture into it. Bake 50 minutes.

Gluten Free & Dairy Free Banana Bread with Walnuts

1 1/4 Cups of rice flour
1 Tbsp. baking powder.
1/2 Tbsp. baking soda.
1/2 Tbsp. Xanthan gum
2/3 Cups sugar
3/4 Tsp. salt
1/3 Cup Margarine
2 Eggs
2 Tbsp. almond milk
1 Cup ripe banana
1/4 Cup chopped nut.

Directions:

Add the Milk with the banana already smushed and set aside. Stir together flour, power, soda and 3/4 tsp salt, and Xathan gum and set aside. In a mixer bowl beat margarine, sugar, eggs (one at a time). Beating until the batter is smooth. Add the banana mixture alternately with flour and finishing with flour and beat until homogenous. Incorporate the walnuts and stir. Pour batter in a lightly greased 8x4x2 inch loaf pan.

Bake at 350f degrees for 60 to 65 minutes, or until toothpick inserted in the center comes out clean. Cool in pan for 10 minutes. Remove from pan; cool.

Cheesecake

CRUST
1 1/4 Cups GRAHAM CRACKER CRUMBS
2 Tbsp. Melted butter.
2 Tbsp. of Sugar
CAKE
2-8 Oz packaged of Cream Cheese (softened)
1 Cup of Sugar
3 Eggs
1 Tbsp. vanilla
2 Tbsp. almond flavoring
1 Pint of Sour cream

Directions:

Grease a 9-inch spring form pan and sprinkle with the crumb's mixture. Pack on bottom and up sides of pan.

Soften cream cheese and beat until fluffy. Gradually add sugar while mixing. Add eggs (1 at a time), beating after each egg. Add flavoring and sour cream.

Bake at 375°F for 30 minutes. Turn oven off but leave the cake in for one hour. Chill and serve.

Gluten & Dairy Free Carrot Cake with Walnuts

CAKE
1 Cup of rice flour
1 Cup of almond flour
1 Tbsp. Xanthan Gum
1 Cup vegetable oil
¼ Cup of almond milk
2 Tsp. baking soda
2 Tsp. baking power
2 Tsp. ground cinnamon
½ Tsp. salt
3 Cup grated carrots.
1 Cup chopped walnuts.

Directions:

Heat the oven to 350°F.

In a bowl, stir the flour, Xanthan gum, baking soda, baking powder, cinnamon, and salt.

In a mixing bowl, beat the eggs until creamy, then add the vegetable oil and almond milk. Add the dry ingredients. When the batter is homogenous, fold in the grated carrots and the walnuts. In a greasy middle-sized Bundt cake pan, pour batter. Place it in the oven for 45 minutes to 1 hour, or until toothpick inserted in the center comes out clean.

Vanilla Pound Cake

250 gm of butter or 1 cup.
2 1/2 Cup sugar
1 Cup of milk
6 Eggs
2 ¾ Cup of all-purpose flour

Directions:

Whisk butter until flurry. Add sugar little by little, then eggs (one at the time). Add milk, alternating with flour and finishing with the flour.

Chocolate Cake with Kirsch

200 gm butter
4 Eggs
½ cup cocoa powder
2 ¾ All-purpose flour
½ Tsp. Baking power

2 ½ cup sugar
1 Cup water
½ Tsp. salt
½ Tsp. baking power
2 Drops of Kirsch

Directions:

Preheat the oven to 350°F. Grease a Bundt cake pan.

Whisk the butter until creamy and fluffy, slowly incorporating the sugar and eggs (1 at a time). In another bowl, mix the baking soda, baking powder, and salt. In a microwave, heat up the water with the cocoa until boiling, then stir into the mixture, adding the 2 drops of kirsch. Add this mixture to the batter, starting with the cocoa mixture and finishing with flour until a homogeneous batter is created. Pour the batter around the Bundt cake pan and leave in the oven for around 45 minutes, or until a bamboo skewer inserted into the cake comes out clean.

Plum Dairy Free Cake

FILLING:
2 lbs. Plum pitted and cut in slices.
1 Cup of Sugar
1 Tbsp. Cinnamon

BATTER:
1 Cup Vegetable oil
½ Cup orange juice
3 Cup All-purpose flour
2 Tsp. vanilla extract
3 Tsp. baking power
1 Tsp. baking soda

TOPPING:
2 Tbsp. Sugar mixer with ground cinnamon

Directions:

Heat the oven to 350°F and grease a 9x3-inch form or tube pan.

Toss the plums with sugar and cinnamon.

Batter

Beat the eggs, sugar, oil, orange juice, and vanilla and mix for a couple of minutes until the batter is creamy, light, and fluffy. In another bowl, sift together the flour, baking soda, and baking powder at a low speed, slowly adding it to the egg mixture. Increase the speed to medium and beat until the ingredients are well combined.

Add 1 to ¼ cups to the prepared pan and top with a third of the plums. Repeat the process several times, ending with a layer of plums on top.

Bake at 350°F for 1 ¼ hour or until a bamboo skewer inserted in the middle of the cake comes out clean.

CHAPTER VI

A Trip to Italy

ROME & PALERMO

My first flight to Italy was memorable because of all the airport aggravation. I took Air Alitalia from JFK to Rome, and my flight was fraught with difficulties. About twenty minutes after we boarded the plane, the pilot announced that there were mechanical difficulties, and we had to vacate the plane and return to the main terminal. We had a three-hour stopover; to compensate us for the inconvenience, we received dinner vouchers. After dinner, we again boarded the plane for the nine-hour flight to Rome. The flight attendants started serving drinks, and I chose a lovely Chianti wine from the Tuscany region of Italy. For dinner, I selected perciatelli pasta with vegetables, a thick, spaghetti-like pasta with holes in the center. After dinner, I was ready for a good night's sleep, and I awoke the next morning when the flight attendants turned on the lights and started serving breakfast. For breakfast, I had orange juice, tea, and a cornetto, an Italian croissant-like pastry filled with hazelnuts and chocolate.

When the plane landed, I prepared to take another plane to Palermo, the capital of the autonomous region of Sicily, an island off the Italian coast. Because of our delay at JFK, unfortunately I missed the flight, and went to the Air Alitalia booth to schedule another flight in the evening. Upon my arrival in Palermo, my family was waiting for me. They drove me via highway A29 in the direction of Trapani-Mazada to San Vito Lo Capo, where I was staying. I could see that Palermo was cuddled up between mountains that spilled into the bays surrounding the city. Palermo was a noble city, and was once the capital of the Roman Empire.

Palermo can thank the ancient Greeks, Arabs, French, and Moors who left their mark on its culture, history, architecture, and especially its gastronomy. Its climate is like North Africa, with intense sun in the summer, giving Sicilian food and produce its bold flavor. Tomatoes are plump, meaty, and have an exquisite, characteristically sweeter smell and taste. Olive oil is more flavorful, fennel tastes more like aniseed, capers are insane, and anchovies and sardines have a wonderful taste fresh from the sea.

You can find plenty of food markets in the streets of Palermo, and quite an experience! The Sicilians are passionate, warm, candid, and are emotional people, and you can literally feel it and hear it as you stroll the streets. In the markets, vendors set up stands in tight, narrow streets leading to a piazza (square). You can find temporary stands at the edges of neighborhoods. The vendors sing in a cacophony of sounds, reciting what they're selling. In these markets, you can buy anything: meat, fish, poultry, cheese, vegetables, bread, desserts, even canned food. Not only can you find raw food, but some stands have grills where the men can grill whatever you desire, much like an American street fair. Fish markets are a sight to behold! The maestros polipari are vendors that sell only tidbits of octopus, like the Japanese with the skill of a samurai. The polipari always have a huge pot, with steaming and boiling water ready to cook the octopus. After they steam the octopuses, they put them on large wooden cutting boards and chop them into delicious bitesized bits. There are also vendors that sell steamed mussels and calamari salads. Vegetable stands have kitchens in the back, with large pots of boiling water to cook vegetables for insalatas cotta or croda (cooked or raw salad). You can get a fresh salad with boiled potatoes, eggs tossed with black olives, capers, onions, fresh olive oil from the region, balsamic vinegar, salt, and pepper. When it's time to leave the market, the vendors express their displeasure over you not buying anything: "Me ne vayo!"

TRIP TO ROME

From Palermo, I took a flight back to Rome. At my arrival I felt very tired, but after resting in the hotel and taking a good nap, I was ready to stay in Rome, and there is not a better way to understand the collage of the Romans, their culture, and gastronomy than visiting the markets. So, Campo de Fiore could not be missed.

Strolling around the market, I found that, besides being a beautiful place, it was very historic, interesting ,and fun. Campo de Fiore is in the historic center of Rome. The piazza was once a field covered with flowers, hence its name "Field of Flowers."

Walking around, I noticed that the Italian cuisine was the least affected from outside influences. To understand the Roman cuisine and be curious enough, I asked a couple of Italian women how they shopped, and to provide me information on some of their Roman dishes. They explained in broken English that basically they shopped for vegetables, meat, produce, fruit, or charcuterie daily, depending on what they cooked each day. They told me that one of the favorite and unforgettable dishes on any Roman table is spaguitti alla carbonara, a total delicacy. The seasoning cannot be missed in Roman cuisine; it is the cornerstone of Roman gsatronomy.

For pepperoncini (red pepper flakes), they use garlic, anchovies and pecorino, with its distinct spicy flavor. Also, they eat a popular lamb: previously milk-fed, and cooking mostly the lungs and liver with artichokes. This dish is called cortadelle de abbacchino con carciofi. Boneless pig is another delicacy, but the favorite Roman dish is porcetta, which is a pig marinated in herbs, pestatta, and more seasonings. The pagliatta with rigatoni is another, which is prepared with veal intestines cooked in their milk, tomato sauce, and ricotta cheese. There's also the famous: saltimbocca alla romana, which is a tender, sliced veal topped with savory prosciutto ham and flavored with very fresh sage. I invite you to give it a try!

If you visit Rome in spring during the months of April and May, you must try the divine, meaty, and tasty artichokes. You would not miss them in any market, restaurant, or in any Roman home. They're a total delicacy!

At night, around the market you will enjoy wonderful restaurants to try any Roman dish or a good cocktail.

Some of the must-see sights in Rome include Fontana dei Trevi, the Coliseum, Vatican City, and the Campo dei Fiori Market, a shopping venue which has streets named for the craftspeople who set up shops there: Via dei Baullari (truck makers), Via dei Cappellari (hatmakers), and Via Giubbonari (jacket makers). If you're an ice cream aficionado, you can go to the nearby Piazza Navona and indulge in an exquisite Italian sorbet or cold gelato.

Now I'd like to recount some other trips I took to other regions of Italy.

TRIP TO NAPLES

From my arrival in Naples, I felt the warm, candid, and emotional people, who try to help others with anything they could need, not even speaking English. Just after strolling around, I loved what I saw: their sense of community and inclusiveness and happy way of life. I heard music escaping from homes, the authentic smell of ragus emanating from windows, happy children playing in the piazzas, laundry hanging from balconies, and more music in piazzas. Naples has a very interesting and rich history, being around 3000 years old. I must recommend visiting Mount Vesubio, Pompei, Centro Storico of Naples, and Capri Island, where you will find designer clothing, handmade leather sandals, Limoncello liqueur—an authentic drink of the region—and the blue Grotto of Capri. Experience the magic of this marvelous, dark cave with super blue waters. Special for Lovers!

Authentic Neapolitan pizza is a specialty of this area, and the Neapolitans are experts in the art of pizza-making: The puffy crust has a very thin center, and they use mozzarella made from water buffalo milk. The marinara sauce is made with raw San Marzano pulp passed through a mill, and it's used sparingly. On the plate, the pizza is cut neatly, and basil is scattered on top. The real secret of Neapolitan pizza lies in the unique flavors of its ingredients.

Pasta is one of the main dishes in the Neapolitan kitchens, and they can thank Marco Polo for bringing it from China to Italy. It's very important in Naples, more than in any other city in Italy, to prepare the pasta al dente, which we can be recognized for its firm texture and for never being overcooked. Otherwise, it wouldn't be edible and appealing. There are infinite pastas, and they mix their pasta with San Marzano tomato. They are juicy and characterized by a distinctive flavor. These tomatoes are grown in the outskirts of the city and are cooked in an earthenware skillet, only for a few minutes in high heat, to thicken the consistency of the sauce, which is served with al dente pasta. In Naples, I tried several pastas: *spaguetti alla salseta d'aglio, vermicelli con le vongole,* and *bucatini alla finta amatriciana*. All were *molto delizioso*!

Let's continue the travels around Italy!

TRIP TO TUSCANY

From Naples, I flew to the region of Tuscany. I found the cities there to be splendid, with the vast, deep, dry hills of vineyards, their marvelous art, atmosphere, culture, and cuisine. For 3,000 years, this region has been a leader in the arts, including the culinary arts. Tuscan eating habits have remained stable through the centuries, and I wanted to discover Tuscan cuisine for myself.

Tuscany is a large region comprised of seacoasts, hills, mountains, plains, cities, suburbs, and villages, all populated by regionalists who have their own approach to cooking, albeit with simplicity. It's centered around a love of wine, bread, and freshly pressed olive oil. Wine is a part of every Tuscan kitchen and table. Whether strong or light, red or white, Tuscans consider wine a flavoring and ingredient, not merely a beverage. A classic, unsalted loaf of bread toasted with garlic oil is the perfect complement to the bold flavors of country ham, sheep's or goat's milk, cheese, and salami. Bread is also a basic ingredient in several popular dishes, such as *ribollita* (a thick, comforting winter soup made from bread, green beans, black cabbage, and extra virgin olive oil) or *panzanella* (a summer salad composed of bread, tomatoes, onions, and oil).

Tuscans are very big on herbs, spices, and vegetables. The main herbs found in Tuscan pantries are parsley, sage, rosemary, thyme, bay leaves, and marjoram. They use garlic, onions, and leeks freely in their cooking, as they believe these vegetables are stimulating and have health and even aphrodisiac benefits. Some popular Tuscan recipes include roasted meats slowly cooked in wine with chopped vegetables, a stew simmering in shallow earthenware casseroles and seasoned with mild fennel, lemon peel, and fixed spices, and an old recipe (before the discovery of America and tomatoes) of braised meats cooked in unripe grape juice and thyme.

Pastas in Tuscan cuisine include *pappardelle* (a centuries-old pasta), *pici* (a thick, fresh spaghetti from Montalcino), *tordelli* (a meat-filled pasta), and ravioli filled with spinach and ricotta.

My favorite city in Tuscany was its capital city, Florence, mainly because of its contribution to Italian and even European gastronomy. When I visited Florence, I noticed their peaches and melons were especially lush, plump, and sweet, and their oysters were a delight to the appetite.

The local Florentines taught me about the important role women played there during the Renaissance. At that time, during the 15th century, most poulterers and greengrocers were women. These women also ran shops selling peacocks, venison, foxes, wild boar, and woodcock, and there were eight women-owned shops that sold flowers and medicinal herbs. When noblewomen from all of Italy and abroad joined the Medici Court, Florentine cooking flourished. These women were good cooks who combined their knowledge of native dishes with local recipes, so a real cuisine was developed and refined. During the Renaissance, the art of entertaining reached its peak, as did these women's dishes and decorations at the Medici.

THE TRIP TO VENEZIA

The cherry on the cream of my trip to Italy was Venice (*Venezia*). It's in northeastern Italy, bordering the Adriatic Sea, and is made up of 118 islands in a lagoon, making it look like its floating on the water There are no roads, only canals. I travelled to the region by bus and took a small fisherman boat to the main island.

Venice is a unique dream, a wonderful city bragging either historically, architecturally or environmentally. It was once the seaport of the medieval era, surrounded by canals that passed through the beautiful, distinctive facades, which are painted with attractive, warm colors and show their beautiful balconies. Agriculturally, Venice has vast, fertile fields that yield the best fresh fruits and vegetables, walnuts, and lush pastures that feed cows, which provide the best milk (used in the famous *Asiago* and *Grana Padano* cheeses). Venetian gastronomy was very much influenced by the Republic of Venice's (Serenissima Republicca Veneta) *"the more serene or sublime"* rule of the domain for over 700 years, which established Venice as the capital of the spice trade. Each region in Italy had its own cuisine, and there was never an excuse to enjoy its succulent dishes using non-indigenous products such as black pepper, cloves, cinnamon, or ginger, because they are frequently used in Venetian cuisine. For example, *gnocchi* is served in a brown butter sauce and garnished with sugar, cinnamon, and smoked dry ricotta.

Venice's reputation as a romantic destination is well deserved. Venice can transport you to another world with its beauty and its atmosphere. You can take a gondola and ride through the Grand Canal, brave the downtown water traffic in a water bus or water taxi, and float around appreciating and delighting in the sight of the balconies holding beautiful flowerpots, or see landmarks like gothic palaces and the well-known Piazza San Marco and Saint Mark's Basilica, a cathedral with breathtaking Byzantine mosaics. It's like taking a trip to Heaven!

ITALY PHOTOS

Italian Gnocchi With Marinara Sauce Only

Mandamento Palazzo Market, Palermo, Sicily

Market Vegetable Stand, Palermo, Sicily

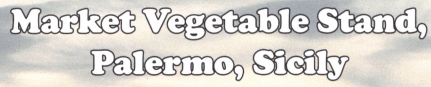

Castellammare del Golfo, Sicily

Custonaci, Sicily

On the street in Trapani, Sicily

Trapani, Sicily

San Vito lo Capo, Italy

ITALIAN RECIPES

Asparagus Risotto

1 lb. asparagus, trimmed and cut into 2" pieces
3 cups canned low sodium chicken broth
2 Tbsp. olive oil 1 medium onion
1 ½ cups of Arborio rice
½ cup dry white wine
6 Tbsp. butter
¾ cup fresh grated parmesan cheese

Directions:

Blanch asparagus pieces in large pot of boiling water for about 2 minutes or until al dente. Place in iced water to cool completely. Drain asparagus well. Bring chicken broth to a simmer in a saucepan. Reduce heat to low to keep broth hot. Heat olive oil in a heavy saucepan over medium heat. Add chopped onion and sauté until clear, about 4 minutes. Add rice and stir for 3 minutes. Add dry white wine and cook until liquid evaporates. Continue cooking until rice is tender, firm in the center of the grain, and forms a creamy mixture. Add 1 cup of chicken broth and stir constantly for about 20 minutes. Remove from heat, add butter, and stir until blended. Stir in parmesan cheese and asparagus. Season risotto with salt and pepper.

Serve immediately.

Baked Eggplant Parmesan

2 eggplant, peeled and cut into ½" slices
1 Tbsp. salt
1 cup Italian-style breadcrumbs
2 eggs, beaten
1 jar tomato sauce with basil
1 cup mozzarella cheese
¼ cup olive oil
¼ tsp. red pepper flakes
Pepper

Directions:

Beat eggs and dip each eggplant slice into the beaten egg mixture. Add pepper and red pepper flakes, then dip each slice into breadcrumbs. Fry in a medium skillet over medium heat until brown. Repeat with remaining slices. Set slices in baking pan with tomato sauce and top with mozzarella cheese. Bake at 350°F for 30 minutes, or until cheese is fully melted.

Caesar Salad

2 small garlic cloves, minced
¼ cup extra virgin olive oil
1 Tsp. anchovy paste
2 egg yolks
2 Tbsp. freshly squeezed lemon juice
½ cup parmesan cheese
1 Tsp. Dijon mustard
Croutons
¼ Tsp. salt
¼ Tsp. pepper
1½ heads of romaine lettuce, washed and torn into bite-sized pieces

Directions:

Beat egg yolks with a steady drizzle of olive oil for about 5 minutes, until forming a mayonnaise. Add garlic, anchovy paste, Dijon mustard, salt, and pepper and toss in the romaine lettuce. Add parmesan cheese and croutons. Serve immediately and place more parmesan on the table.

Chicken Marsala with Mushrooms

4 eggs
5 Tbsp. butter
1 cup seasoned breadcrumbs
1 Tbsp. of fresh sage, chopped
¼ Tsp. of salt
Lemon slices (garnish)
Chicken broth
10 oz. mushrooms, trimmed and thinly sliced
1/8 Tsp. pepper
1 cup all-purpose flour
2 Tbsp. olive oil
1 cup marsala wine
1 Tsp. lemon juice
Parsley (garnish)
4 skinless boneless chicken breast halves

Directions:

In a medium bowl, beat eggs with salt and pepper. Set aside. Have two plates ready, one each for flour and breadcrumbs. Dip each chicken breast half in the egg mixture, then in flour, then the egg mixture again, and finally in breadcrumbs. Repeat until all chicken breasts are done.

In a heavy medium skillet, on medium heat, melt butter, oil, and sage. Fry each chicken breast until golden brown. Repeat for all chicken breasts. Set chicken breasts in a baking pan. Use remaining juices from skillet to sauté mushrooms. Pour some melted butter from the skillet on top of chicken breasts. Add mushrooms, lemon juice, chicken broth, and marsala wine. Bake at 350°F for 50 minutes. Garnish with lemon slices and parsley.

Eggplant Rollatini

Nonstick olive oil spray
2 large eggs
2 2/3 cups parmesan cheese
18 eggplant slices, ¼" thick
3 cups mozzarella cheese, coarsely grated
1 ¼ cups ricotta cheese
¾ cup fresh basil leaves, chopped
3 cups high-quality marinara sauce

Directions:

Preheat oven to 350°F. On a baking sheet, sprinkle eggplant slices with salt and roast them until tender. Spray a 13" x 9" x 2" glass baking dish with olive oil. For the filling, mix the cheeses, eggs, basil, salt, pepper, and a pinch of red pepper flakes. Divide filling among the eggplant slices (about 3 tbsp. per slice), and spread evenly. Starting with one short end, roll up the eggplant slices around the filling. Arrange rolls, seam side down, in the prepared baking dish. (Note: can be made one day ahead and chill.)

Spoon marinara sauce on top of rolls and sprinkle with some parmesan cheese. Bake uncovered for about 30 minutes, or until mozzarella is melted and rolls are well heated inside. Serve hot and garnish with basil leaves.

Fettuccine with Tomato Sauce, Cauliflower & Anchovies

1 large cauliflower (about 2 ½ lbs.)
¼ cup water
1/8 Tsp. saffron
¼ cup pine nuts
1/3 cup extra virgin olive oil
1 lb. gemelli (dry pasta)
1 onion, finely chopped
8 large, fresh bay leaves
3 small anchovies, chopped
1 ½ Tbsp. kosher salt
¼ cup golden raisins
½ cup grated pecorino cheese (plus more for table)
1 cup tomato sauce

Directions:

Fill a large pot with 6 qt. water, add salt, and heat until boiling. Trim cauliflower and cut florets and stem into 1-inch pieces. Rinse pieces and blanch them in boiling water until slightly al dente, about 5 minutes. Lift cauliflower pieces from pot with a spatula, drain briefly, and drop into a bowl. Pour 1 cup of hot water in a bowl and soak saffron. Pour olive oil in a big skillet, put in onion until browned (about 5 minutes), then stir in chopped anchovies.

When anchovies are melted in the oil, pour in water infused with saffron, add tomato sauce, and cook for 10 minutes. Add cauliflower, raisins, and pine nuts. Toss everything together, cover pan, and cook for a couple of minutes.

Meanwhile, drop dry pasta into a pot of boiling water and cook for about 10 minutes until al dente. Uncover the skillet and let the water evaporate until vegetables are caramelized. Lift pasta from water, drop directly into skillet, and toss with vegetables. On top, add crushed bay leaves, sprinkle with pecorino, and drizzle with olive oil. Serve right away, passing more grated cheese around the table.

Linguine with Shrimp & Scallops

1 lb. shrimp, deveined (keep shell)
1 lb. prepared scallops
2 Tbsp. butter
2 shallots, finely chopped
1 cup dry white wine or vermouth
1 ½ cups water
1 lb. linguine
2 Tbsp. olive oil
2 Tbsp. chives, finely sliced
Salt and pepper

Directions:

Melt butter in a medium skillet. Add shallots and cook over medium heat until light brown. Add shrimp shells, and stir constantly for about a minute. Pour in wine or vermouth and cook, stirring for one minute. Add water and bring to a boil. Reduce heat and simmer until half of liquid evaporates. Over high heat, bring a pot of water to a boil. Add pasta. Cook for 8-10 minutes until tender or al dente.

Meanwhile, heat olive oil in a medium skillet. Add shrimp and scallops until shrimp changes color and scallops are opaque. Strain the shell stock and pour into skillet. Drain pasta, add to stock, and add chives. Season with salt and pepper to taste. Toss well and serve immediately.

Janisa's Homemaden Nepolitarian Marinara Sauce

- 1 Big onion
- 3 Cloves garlic
- 2 Cans San Marzano tomatoes
- 4 Basil leaves
- 1 Tbsp. salt

Directions:

Add olive oil to an earthenware pot, along with sauteed, minced garlic and cut onions. Cook until caramelized, then add San Marzano tomatoes, basil, and salt. Let simmer until thick on a very low flame for about 1 hour. TUTTO A TAVOLA A MANGARE

Janisa's Perfect Nepolitanian Pizza

1 Package active dry yeast
1 Tsp. sugar
1 Cup warm water
2 ½ Cups bread flour
2 Tbsp. olive oil
1 Tsp. salt

For The Marinara Sauce

1 Big onion
3 Cloves garlic
2 Cans San Marzano tomatoes
4 Basil leaves
1 Tbsp. salt
3 Tbsp. Olive oil

Directions:

Preheat oven to 350°F.

In a bowl, dissolve the yeast with the sugar and let it sit for 10 minutes. Stir in flour, salt, and olive oil and mix until smooth. Let it sit for 10 minutes. Use a floured flat surface to pad down the dough into a flat, round shape. Transfer dough to a pizza pan, then top with marinara sauce and fresh buffalo mozzarella cheese. (Veggies optional). Bake for 30- 35 minutes.

Pan Fried Fillet Of Sole with Lemon Butter Sauce In A Polenta Bed

8 sole fillets
½ cup flour
½ Tsp. seasoning salt
¼ Tsp. fresh ground pepper
7 Tbsp. butter
¼ cup fresh lemon juice
2 Tbsp. parsley leaves, freshly chopped
1 cup instant polenta

Directions:

Mix flour, seasoning salt, and pepper in a shallow dish. Dredge fish fillets in the flour mixture. Heat a large skillet over high heat. Add about 3 tbsp. butter. Sauté fillets in two batches until thoroughly cooked. Transfer to a plate and keep warm. Add the remaining 4 tbsp. butter and cook until golden. Add lemon juice, bring to a boil, and add parsley.

Preheat oven to 350°F. Slice instant polenta into 1-inch thick round slices and cook for 20 minutes. Place polenta on a plate and sole fillets on top. Pour lemon juice on top and garnish with parsley.

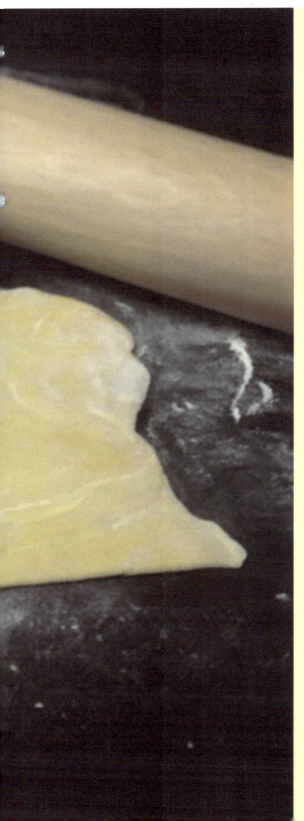

Pasta Dough For Ravioli

1 ½ cups white bread flour, plus extra for dusting
2 eggs, slightly beaten
1 Tbsp. olive oil Pinch of salt

Directions:

Sift flour and salt onto a work surface and make a well in the center. Pour eggs and olive oil into the well. Using one hand, gradually incorporate the flour into the liquid. Knead the dough on a floured work surface until dough is smooth to the touch. Wrap dough with plastic wrap paper and let stand for 30 minutes; this makes dough more elastic. Roll out or feed through a pasta machine.

Pumpkin Ravioli with Tomatoes & Ricotta

1 egg
4 garlic cloves
4 cups pumpkin flesh
4 sun-dried tomatoes
All-purpose flour (dusting)
(plus 2 Tbsp. oil from tomatoes)

½ cup ricotta cheese
1 Tbsp. rosemary, chopped.
Pasta dough (previous recipe)
Pepper

Directions:

Preheat oven to 400°F. Wrap garlic in aluminum foil and roast in oven for 10 minutes. In a food processor, blend garlic, sun-dried tomatoes, ricotta, rosemary, salt, and pepper, until it forms a mesh. Divide pasta dough as follows: wrap half in plastic wrap and put aside. Roll out the other half on a lightly floured surface to form a rectangle 1/16-inch to 1/8-inch thick. Cover with a damp dish towel. Remove half of the plastic and roll out to the same size. Place small mounds (about 1 tsp. each) of the pumpkin filling in rows 1½" apart. Brush the edges between the mounds with a beaten egg.

Remove dish towel from the other half, place the pasta on top of the halves with the filling, and press down firmly between pockets of filling to push out air bubbles. Use a pasta wheel or sharp knife to cut into squares. Place on a floured dish towel and let stand for 1 hour. Bring a large pan of salted water to a boil. Add ravioli, return to boil, and cook for 3-4 minutes until tender. Toss with oil from tomatoes and serve immediately.

Truffle Risotto

6-8 cups water
4 Tbsp. extra virgin olive oil
2 cups onions, chopped.
1 Tsp. salt (add more to taste)
2 cups arborist or carnaroli rice
1 cup white wine

For finishing:
6 Tbsp. butter (in 1 Tbsp. pieces)
½ cup freshly grated Grana Padano or Parmigiano Reggiano cheese
White truffle, 1 oz. or larger, brushed clean.

Directions:

Heat water in pot almost to a boil. Cover and keep it very hot on the stove, near the risotto pan. In the risotto pan, pour in onion, olive oil, and ½ tsp. of salt and set over medium heat. Stir well as the onion gets translucent; cook until brownish, about 8 minutes. Pour in rice, raise the heat, and stir rice and onions continuously, toasting the rice grains until they make a clicking sound; do not brown them. Pour in wine, and keep stirring for another couple of minutes, until moisture has evaporated and rice is totally dry.

Immediately pour 2 cups of simmering water into the rice until covered. Lower heat. Cook, stirring steadily, until the water is fully absorbed, about 4 to 6 minutes. Quickly pour in more water to cover the rice, add another ½ tsp. salt, and keep stirring as the rice swells and releases its starches and a thick, creamy mixture starts to form. When the water is absorbed, add another cup of water (making a total of about 6 cups of water), until risotto is perfectly cooked, al dente and creamy. Quickly drop the butter pieces into the saucepan and stir constantly until fully blended. On the top, stir in grated cheese and shaved truffle flakes. Serve immediately, as the heat releases the aroma of the truffle.

Other Recipe

- 1 large cauliflower 2 1/2 lbs.
- 1/3 cup extra virgin oil
- 3 small anchovies chopped
- 1/4 cup of pine nuts
- 1/4 water
- 8 large fresh basil leaves
- 1/2 cup grated pecorino, plus more for the table.
- 1/8 Tsp. of saffron
- 1 onion finely chopped.
- 1/4 cup of golden raisins.
- 1 cup tomato sauce
- 1 lbs. gemelli (dry pasta)
- 1 1/2 Tbsp. of kosher salt

Directions:

Fill the large pot with 6 quarter of water, add 1 1/2 tablespoon of salt, and heat until boiling. Trim the cauliflower and cut all the florets and tender stems into 1-inch pieces. Rinse the pieces and blanch them in the boiling water until slightly al dente, about 5 minutes. Lift the cauliflower from the pot with a spider, drain briefly, and drop the pieces into a bowl. Pour one cup of the hot water in a bowl and soak the saffron. Pour the 1/3 cup of olive oil in a big skillet, add the onion, and cook until brownish, about 5 minutes. Then stir in the chopped anchovies.

When the anchovies melt in the oil, pour the infused water with the saffron, tomato sauce, cauliflower, raisins, and pine nuts. Toss everything together, cover the pan, and cook for a couple of minutes. Meanwhile, drop the dry pasta into the big pot of boiling water and cook for about 10 minutes until al dente. Uncover the skillet and let the water evaporate, until the vegetables caramelize. Lift the pasta from the water and drop it directly into the skillet. Toss the pasta with vegetables. Add the crushed bay leaves on top, sprinkle with pecorino, and drizzle with olive oil. Serve right away, passing more grated cheese at the table.

ITALIAN DESSERT

Italian Blueberry Polenta Dessert

1 ½ cups sugar, divided.
3 cups blueberries
2 large eggs
Zest of 1 large orange, finely grated.
2/3 cup orange juice
2/3 cup olive oil (not extra virgin) or sunflower oil
½ cup regular or instant polenta
1 ¼ cups all-purpose flour
1 Tsp. baking powder
½ Tsp. salt

Directions:

Preheat oven to 350°F. Grease and line base and sides of a 9-inch square cake pan with baking parchment paper and grease the parchment. Sprinkle 1/3 cup sugar over base of pan and cover evenly with blueberries.

In a large mixing bowl, combine eggs, 1 cup of sugar, and orange zest. Whisk until pale and thick. Add orange juice and oil and whisk until blended. In a separate bowl, whisk together polenta, flour, baking powder, and salt.

Add flour mixture to egg mixture and whisk until smooth. Pour into prepared pan. Bake for about 45-50 minutes, until golden brown and springy to the touch and a toothpick inserted near the center comes out clean. Cool cake on a rack for about 5 minutes. Carefully invert cake onto serving plate.

Italian Profiteroles Dessert

1 cup cold water
4 Tbsp. (1/2 stick) butter
2 ½ Tsp. sugar
Pinch of salt
1 cup all-purpose flour
3 eggs
Whipping cream
Chocolate fudge

Directions:

In a saucepan, bring water, butter, sugar, and salt to a boil. Add flour and stir until dough is firm. Remove from heat and place dough in a medium bowl. Add 1 egg and stir until completely mixed. Repeat the same for the other 2 eggs. Let mixture set and cool for a few minutes and place in a decorating bag. On top of a baking sheet lined with parchment paper, make flowers, leaving at least 2" between them. Bake at 350°F for 30 minutes. When cool, cut them in the middle, fill with whipping cream, and put chocolate fudge on top.

CHAPTER VII

A Trip To Spain

A DASH OF HISTORY

Spain is a cultural mosaic, including seventeen autonomous regions. It is situated in the southwest of Europe bathing between by the Atlantic Sea and the Mediterranean Sea. Because of its geographic location and history, this has permitted influence on the Spanish cuisine. Spain's capital is Madrid, which is the home of the royal palace, and home to the best recognized Spanish arts. Geographically, its varied climate and topography—from the highest and harshest mountains in Europe to the most beautiful tropical islands—has given rise to a great wealth of fish and produce. The Iberian Peninsula is an eclectic melting pot of culture and customs. Historically speaking, Spanish food originated from the Romans. They were experienced agriculturists and cooks who knew how to cultivate foodstuffs, such as wheat, olive oil, wine, and salted fish. After the Romans stepped foot in Hispania, they realized the treasure they'd found in the Hispania lands necessary for the cultivation and supply of basic food. Later, the Romans incorporated cereals into the Mediterranean diet, mostly bread-making, which was a total delight in their art of cooking. Bread was a common ingredient or base in many dishes, such as Spanish garlic soup, or as a thickener in *gazpacho*, a soup with raw vegetables served cold.

The Romans cultivated the wild olive trees on a grand scale, making Spain the foremost supplier and consumer of olive oil. "Chefs and food critics proudly declared that Spanish olive oil was the primary medium for cooking and frying foods, as it provided flavor, a smooth texture, and unity for uncooked ingredients, richness for cooked dishes, thickness for stews, and protection for roasts." In fact, the Romans were the ones responsible for introducing the cooking methods of roasting, broiling, and grilling, which are all still in use.

After Germany invaded Spain around 476 A.D., the Roman Empire collapsed and the Spanish cuisine took on its own international character. The Visigoths introduced livestock farming, and the Iberian pig has since become one of the prime elements of Spanish stock raising. *Jamón Iberico de Bellota* is ham from pigs fed only with acorns during their final period, giving it a unique, distinct flavor.

During the Medieval Era, Spain started producing local cheeses. However, they were unnoticed due to lack of sanitation standards. Nowadays, after years of rigid methods of pasteurization and proper methods of guaranteeing areas of origin, the cheeses in Spain are in large-scale production, and they are famous all over the world, like the Manchego Cheese!

Perhaps Arabs who migrated to Spain offered the biggest influence on Spanish cuisine. They saw the lands as a paradise, able to transform arid soil into the most fertile crops, such as citrus fruits, rice, eggplants, and sugar cane, and they were instrumental in the widespread use of poultry, rice, and fried foods. They also introduced spices, such as saffron, cinnamon, cumin, cilantro, and mint. Arab ideas about food became totally assimilated with Spanish cuisine; however, during the expulsion of Arabs out of Spain and the hostility of anything linked to the Arab culture, Arabs dishes and spices were recognized as solely Spanish.

In 1492, after the discovery of America and the reunification of Spain following the conquest of Granada, the Last Arab Kingdom gave to Spanish cuisine a revolution in appearance, touch, and flavor. This was during the monarchy of the Catholics, King Fernando and Queen Isabella. The Arabs brought new foods into Spain from India and Mexico: tomatoes, bell peppers, subterranean potatoes, black bitter cocoa, sweet vanilla, and paprika. These foods were considered fanciful eccentricities (sometimes even dangerous!), but they led to the creation of many new dishes. The practice of curing pork meat with paprika resulted in the famous *chorizo* sausage, and paprika was used in other new dishes, such as *pisto* (a vegetable stew) and *tortilla de patatas* (a golden potato omelet). Cocoa brought from Mexico (mixed with sugar) was deemed so expensive that it should only be used by royalty, perhaps for occasions like a royal wedding. It's said that in 1660, Maria Teresa, daughter of Philip IV of Spain, took chocolate with her to Paris when she married Louis XIV of France.

During the Bronze Age, Spaniards starting using *potajes* (hotpots) for cooking. Although it was more sophisticated than roasting, all it required was a fire-resistant pole to haul the pot over the fire and allow it to be removed to prevent burning. One special type of potaje, a stewing pot (known as *la olla*), is made of clay, and is narrower at the top and wide as a big belly at the bottom. Potajes are tedious because they require much stirring. All the ingredients are seasoned and combined in water to soften them, making them digestible and delicious!

ELEMENTS OF SPANISH CUISINE

Appetizers (*Aperitivos y Tapas*): These are miniature, elegant, self-serve dishes: a total piece of art, designed to stimulate the appetite for the large midday meal, basically a dish of the upper classes. Tapas constitute small meals, and tapas dining is a trend. One of the pleasures of living in Spain is going on a *tapeo*, an informal social gathering where people move leisurely from bar to bar to sample tapas, complemented by beverages, usually *Rioja* red wine.

Salads: In Mediterranean countries, there's a vast array of fresh produce and ingredients to prepare delicious salads. They can be made with both cooked and raw vegetables, but are always served cold. Salads were originally intended to be an inexpensive option for the lower classes, or an alternative to meat, but nowadays salad is served after cold fruit and before the main course of meat, or at *meriendas* (afternoon tea or snack) at home or in the country. A very popular Spanish salad is *ensalada mixta*, which is prepared by mixing lettuce, tomatoes, onions, olives, canned asparagus tips, canned tuna, a hard-boiled egg, olive oil, vinegar, salt, and pepper.

Soup: The Spaniards have always been fond of soup, so much so that it's even mentioned in Spanish literature. Whether simple or elaborate, it's part of every Spanish home and occasion. There are many slang terms associated with it: *La Sopa Boba* ("silly soup") is soup provided by religious communities to feed the poor; *La Sopa Estudiantes* is soup that's a staple of university students, which they're known to complain about. Because soup is considered easier to digest than other foods, two kinds of soups are made and served specifically to sick people: *puchero para dolientes y enfermos* (invalid soup) and *puchero reconfortante* (comforting soup). In Spain, soup can be made with meat, fish, or vegetables, and seafood is used for flavor in broth and stocks. *Medunilla* soup contains ham, chicken liver, chicken breast, and a hard-boiled egg; marinara soup is tomato-based, and often contains shellfish.

A Spanish specialty is the gazpacho, or cold vegetable soup. There are many types of gazpachos in terms of vegetables used and consistency. In *The Heritage of Spanish Cooking,* authors Alicia Rios and Lourdes March write that gazpacho originally referred to a "rustic yet creative combination of ingredients in a mortar, improvised with whatever was available, but always based on the constant components of bread, water, oil, salt, vinegar, and garlic." Preparing gazpacho is an example of real culinary alchemy, or mixing varied ingredients for a magical cold soup outcome. Olive oil is the first ingredient, then salt (to break up fiber from the vegetables and to extract the vegetable juice), and finally, garlic. Vinegar is used to create a thin, refreshing gazpacho that's perfect for a hot summer day.

My trip to Spain started with a nine-hour flight from JFK to Barajas International Airport in Madrid, Spain. From there, I traveled to several other cities, each with their own distinct culture and cuisine. Let me take you on the journey!

MADRID

In 1561, Madrid was chosen by King Phillip II, making Madrid the capital of Spain. For quite a long time, Madrid was just a province, and its industrialization began late in Spain and started first in neighboring communities like Basque and Catalonia. Until the end of the Spanish Civil War, it was an administrative capital inhabited by bureaucrats. After General Franco's dictatorship, Madrid experienced a renaissance and became an authentic, elegant European metropolis. It was the seat of two royal dynasties, the House of Hapsburg (Austria), and later the House of Bourbon (France). Madrid was considered both *corte* and *villa*, a court and a small town at the same time.

Madrid's culinary culture became a dichotomy: simple but robust cooking by ordinary people, but at the same time it was influenced by the refined, aristocratic cooking of the Hapsburg Court and its master chefs. The Bourbons imparted a French style to their cooking. People from other provinces and countries brought their culinary traditions to Madrid, such as fine seafood from Cantabria and Galicia, and chocolate from Mexico, and they were welcomed by the chefs Madrilenôs. This is how Madrid's gastronomy rose to world class status, and it is known, distinguished, and recognized all around the world. Also, you can stroll around Madrid's enormous parks and visit the majestic Royal Palace, La Zarzuela, with its impressive 3,000 guest rooms. In Madrid, do not miss the wonderful museums, taverns, coffee shops, and restaurants that make the city roar.

I visited Puerta Del Sol Square in Madrid, which sits at kilometer zero in the center, a place which marks the distances to every road and city in Spain. While walking there, you get an overview of the whole country, because in the bars and taverns there, you're surrounded by immigrants like Galicians, Andalusians, or Basques, who offer fare typical of their native regions. My hotel was near some tourist attractions in Madrid:

La Plaza de España, a large square featuring a monument of Spanish novelist, poet, and playwright, Miguel de Cervantes Saavedra, and El Corte Inglés, a store like Lord&Tailor in America, where you can find the latest fashion trends, brand name couture, electronics, home décor, books, everything imaginable.

Before starting to tour the city, I stopped for breakfast in a cafeteria. In Spain, "*desayunar*" (breakfast) "is a social act," taking place in different locations (depending on social class and circumstances). It's rarely at home. Most Spaniards drink fresh brewed coffee, black or with milk, but some go to the corner and wake up to a glass of aniseed shot—in Spain, this doesn't make you an alcoholic! The majority prefer pastries and sweets, particularly deep-fried *churros* and *porra*. Croissants are also available. Another popular snack is *tosta a la plancha* (a loaf of white bread toasted on the grill) with butter and marmalade. After a few hours of work, Madrileños gather in the cafes to discuss soccer matches and TV programs, indulge in some *café con leche* (white coffee), sweet bread, and fresh-squeezed orange juice. Workers customarily order a *bocadillo* (a sandwich roll filled with ham, tortilla, or cheese) with wine or beer.

If you are curious about the bullfights (the *corrida*), there is no a better place to enjoy them. Bullfights are ritualized stories between a man and woman kept apart by faith. It is a didactic drama seen by connoisseurs and Spaniards alike, an intimate tragedy about a female and her power, seduction, and passion over the male, who finally pays for his insatiable desire with death. Bullfighting is a longstanding national pleasure, hobby, and celebration in Madrid, which blends artistry, tradition, entertainment, and industry, representing a quite moving portrayal of its economy. The bullfights are governed by strict rules: they start with the Matador's salute, lifting the handkerchief, the sound of the trumpets, and the march of the Paso Doble. The spectators are very knowledgeable about corrida and are very critical of the event, and they cheer and complain at the same time. After the bullfight is over, they meet at a tavern to have a glass of wine and discuss the fight.

You can also enjoy the the thirty days of San Isidro Féria in Madrid. Aficionados go to the *ruedo* (bull arena) with their *peña* (group of fellow enthusiasts), and the women wear real Flamenco dresses.

Madrid, Spain

ANDALUSIA (SEVILLE/CÓRDOBA/GRANADA)

From my hotel, I took a taxi to the Madrid Atocha Train Station in the center of Madrid, by the southern end of El Paseo del Prado. I was traveling from Madrid to the autonomous community of Andalusia, which has eight provinces, including Seville (its capital), Córdoba, and Granada. At the train station, an agent explained to me that trains to any destination in Andalusia are comfortable and pleasant. Passengers have plenty of room to move, stretch, and chat with other passengers while admiring the beautiful country scenery. The AVE trains to Seville and Córdoba are very modern, high-speed trains that travel at a rate of about 93 mph. I took an AVE speed train to Seville, and noticed pine, cork, and oak woods alternating with dry, dusty steppes, sand dunes, and mountains. Seville's extremely diverse landscapes and climate zones are a perfect illustration of the charms of Andalusia.

For 800 years, the Arabs and Moors ruled Andalusia. They were an advanced civilization, and they imprinted their marks upon Andalusia's architecture, irrigation system, music, crafts, and cuisine, more so than any other region in Spain. The Arabs were responsible for bringing pomegranates, citrus fruits, figs, and melons to Andalusia, where they flourished in this land of Mediterranean sun. In Andalusian cuisine, the Arabs creatively combined meat and fish with fruits and herbs. These highly healthy, imaginative, sweet dishes are still cooked and served in Andalusian homes today. Personally, I feel that Andalusian cuisine lacks finesse because of its emphasis on solid, basic foods. Typical daily dishes include meat, fish, seafood, and exquisite ham and sausage combined with vegetables. But if you add a glass of sherry, the world-famous wine from this region, any meal is complete!

Before leaving Andalusia, I did some sightseeing in Granada. Like Madrid, Granada is known for its breathtaking sights and attractions, such as the Alhambra, the Cathedral, and Plaza Nueva, and I spent a long day wandering down Granada's small streets and picturesque parks. I then took a taxi to the Granada train station (situated where the Calle de Halcon and Calle Doctor Jaime Garcia Royo converge) and bought a night ticket back to Madrid—much cheaper than a day ticket. From Madrid, I took another AVE speed train to Barcelona, and two hours and forty-five minutes later, I arrived at the Barcelona Sants railway station near Plaça dels Països Catalans.

CATALONIA (BARCELONA)

Barcelona is the capital and one of the provinces of the autonomous community of Catalonia. Barcelona is a melting pot region, attracting settlers from France, Italy, and other parts of Spain, including the south of Spain and Andalusia. Barcelona has a mild climate, and is now one of the cosmopolitan cities with the best quality of life.

The geography of Catalonia ranges from stiff mountains with rushing torrents in the north, beautiful dry plains with a continental climate in the south, and is edged by of the intense blue and shining Mediterranean Sea.

After getting familiar with the surroundings, and especially with the Catalans, I noticed that Catalans were spontaneous, a little complex, and that they suffered from contradictions. This is why it is well said that Catalans have an amazing common sense, which is called seny. One of the ways to know Barcelona is to meet its people and their creativity: to get close to them.

Catalans enthusiastically embrace their diverse way of life, making the land a cradle of unrealistic imagination, which has been said to either "drive people mad or create genius," such as the surrealist painter Salvador Dali, the architect Antonio Gaudi, or the opera singer Monsserat Caballe. The Barcelonians are fierce lovers of sports, and are especially strong patrons of the Barcelona soccer team.

Barcelona is well known for its regional healthy cuisine based on a Mediterranean diet, which reflects the varied characteristics of their land and people. Catalans have perfected the art and chemistry of blending cuisine from the mountains (meat and poultry) and the sea (fish and seafood). When touring around Catalonia, I saw in the distance stone farmhouses where cooks started the culinary tradition of meticulously combining exotic ingredients. The result: chicken with gambas (shrimp), and rabbit cooked to perfection with langostinos (prawns), the latter being rooted in Roman times and novel influences. A classic Catalan recipe is mar i muntanya (surf and turf), a combination of chicken and shrimp. In Barcelona, a not-to-be-missed delicacy is roasted wild duck.

In Barcelona, I visited a must-see venue: the great Basilica Sagrada Familia, a large Roman Catholic church designed by the famed Catalan architect Antoni Gaudi. But since mine was mainly a culinary journey, the highlight of my trip was a visit to the beautiful Mercat de Sant Josep de la Boqueria, commonly known as La Boqueria. This market is a treasure trove for everything the culinary-minded could desire, located close to where people live. It carries the finest products—like the best shrimp and freshest catches of the day—in infinite range and variety. In the spring, Spanish setas (mushroom hunters) with their freshness and perfect aroma bring their best commodities to town, such as mushroom truffles, and chefs from Barcelona's top restaurants come to pick up their treasures to create Catalonia's varied cuisine. In La Boqueria, you can find produce, vegetables, charcuterie, cheeses, or sit in small bars or restaurants for drinks and tapas. If you need to wield your cooking knives, there is not a better place to bring them than the market, where you will find amazing people who have worked in the market for decades and continue to demonstrate their arts, like wielding their sharp knives to perfection to slice tuna. Stand owners like to narrate the market's fascinating history. One historical fact is that the market was originally on a narrow street called Promenade Las Ramblas, which is now perpendicular to La Boqueria. It is well known as Las Ramblas Boulevard. Las Ramblas was where the farmers sold produce and vegetables at the city gate. The name boqueria means "where goat meat is sold." If you collect the famous Lladro, beautiful porcelain, you will find the unique Catalan Lladro store in Las Ramblas Boulevard.

One day I was invited to have merienda (a light meal) with some friends, and when their children came home from the school, they were served pa amb tomàquet (tomato bread). It's sandwich bread soaked in juice from small, fresh, deeply flavored tomatoes, with a few drops of olive oil and salt. It's eaten with cheese, smoked ham, regional sausages, or Spanish tortillas. This is the simplest dish in Catalonia, but one with symbolic significance: it transports adults back to their childhood, where they all used to grow these tomatoes and eat tomato bread after school.

We now know that Marco Polo brought noodles and pasta from China to Italy; however, the Arabs brought them to Spain, and the Italian and Swiss in Spain incorporated them into their cooking in Barcelona. Pasta is a large part of Catalan cuisine, perhaps more than in the rest of Spain. The exquisite cannelloni alla Catalana is one of the dishes using pasta, with a touch of the Catalan cuisine.

In Catalonia, the proper way to start or end a meal is with a cool glass of Catalan cava, a world-famous sparkling wine made by the méthode champenoise, which uses fermentation and maturity in the bottle to enhance flavor.

If you love desserts, the hallmark dessert dish of Catalonia is crema Catalana, like the French crème brûlée, which is made by mixing egg yolks, milk, sugar, and a touch of cinnamon and lemon zest.

Finally, you must enjoy the beaches in Barcelona, which are quiet, with temperatures that allow you to bathe from the autumn to the spring. One of the famous beaches in Barcelona is La Playa Barceloneta, which is edged by the Mediterranean Sea. You can also enjoy the breezy boulevard that allows you to walk along the beach.

Barcelona Photos

**Barcelona Skyline
(includes Port Vell, Sangrada Familia
& Torre Agbar)**

La Boqueria in Barcelona

Barcelona, Spain

Plaza de Cataluna, Barcelona Spain

Basilica De La Sagrada Familia

Architecture Of Barcelona

Trip to La Coruña, province of Galicia Spain

La Coruña is in the northwest of Spain, bathed by the Adriatic Ocean and surrounded by the coast. It's one the most elegant cities in Spain, and is part of the rich historical and autonomous community of Galicia. La Coruña is a port city of fishermen, and its main language is Gallego, although some people speak Castellano and many books are written in that language. Galicia's population, according to the last survey in 2021, is around 112,000 people, and it's distributed between the main communities in Galicia: La Coruña, Santiago de Compostela, and Ferrol.

The old town of La Coruña is modern, and offers beautiful monumental landmarks, giving tourists the excuse to enlighten their eyes and admire the spectacular edifices with enchanting, pleasant walks around the city, like the walk around the famous Plaza de Maria Pita. The square resemble medieval times, and it is a neurological, elegant, and poetic square located in the heart of the old city. It takes its name from a sixteenth century female Galician hero.

The square is surrounded by classical lamps posts, and it is always delightful to experience a coffee overlocking La Coruña's town hall. This building has a more modern style , since it was built in the twentieth century.

There are many other places to appreciate, and it will be always a good choice to stop and try many of the eateries, pulperias, restaurants, taverns, and bars to taste authentic Galician food.

The exquisite gastronomy is based according to where you are located around La Coruña, and it offers a variety of fresh food and a good quality of caught fish. Many are marinated in spices and condiments with vegetables, sardines, and delicious soups. Potaje gallego which is a rich soup cooked with Gallegan chorizo, or pork with spices, vegetables, shellfish, and fish on the grill. Moreover, La Coruña also delights us with dishes of marine cuts, for all lovers of seafood. Pulpo a La Gallega (octopus a La Gallega) is a typical dish. The octopus is cut in little bites and served with olive oil and peppers.

There is also empanadas Gallegan, which are filled either with meat, cod, fish, or octopus, or pimiento al padron (peppers al padron). These peppers are fried or grilled and served with olive oil and coarse salt.

Furthermore, you can stroll the narrow streets and find souvenirs and luxury stores, or find the Jardines Mendez Nuñez, where you may sit and enjoy the view while having a sunbath, with a delightful breeze in the summer. Also, the province provides you with lovely places to fall in love like cliffs, and majestic places of authentic enchantment.

Be sure to visit the beautiful and elegant Riazor beach, which it is located in the center of the city. It's one of the most elegant in Spain, or so the monument of human patrimony (La Torre de Hercules) declared. It is a tower that has been operating since ancient times, with an amazing view of the city and the sea.

If you are a beer lover, do not miss the opportunity to discover "The Art of Beer Making" at the magnificent Museum of Mega Mundo Estrella Galicia. It is a unique experience of learning the whole process while using all your senses, delighting the palate until it drops with different sorts of beers directly from the maestros.

Another must-visit place is Costa de Morte, It's a magical place where you can relax, with its cascade of corners filled with exquisite history and gorgeous maritime environments. Costa de Morte consists of Fisterra, Cabo Vilan, Tourinan, Punta Nariga, and Rias Baixas.

A Trip To La Coruña

A TRIP TO PALMA DE MALLORCA

Palma de Mallorca is in the western Mediterranean and belongs to the Islas Baleares. Palma de Mallorca is known as "Palma," and its capital is Mallorca (Majorca).

Majorca is a marvelous and enchanted island. I really think my description of this beautiful island falls short compared to its magnificence. I immediately fell in love with the island. It is a resort city, and is a main destination of the very wealthy, actors, actresses, Nordics, and Germans who own amazing properties on the island.

I flew—seven hours direct fly—from NY JFK to Barcelona, flying with IBERIA airline, which is the main Spanish Airline, and as I always think of good food, I found that the food during the flight was very appealing compared with many other airlines. The flight from Barcelona to Palma de Mallorca was with Air Europa. This flight is very short; you ascend, and a few minutes later, the captain announces you're descending.

Arriving at the Airport of Sant Son Joan of Mallorca, after collecting your luggage, you can take a bus from the small airport to the main center of Palma de Mallorca, "Plaza de España" (Square), taking the bus number # 1, which is very inexpensive, costing around €3. If you decide to take a taxi instead, it's around €20. But if you are very tired from the trip, I recommend this last option.

La Plaza de España is where all the transportation converges, either taxes, buses, or the Intermodal station, which is where the main lines from EMT stop. It can take you to every little corner of Mallorca.

When I arrived at Plaza de España, I was amazed, seeing that in this main square you can find American food chains, like Taco Bell and McDonald's. In the corner overlooking the avenue, you can find a café, where I tried, for the first time, the Mallorcan coffee latte maquiatto, a delicious, fresh-squeezed orange juice, and a bocadillo (sandwich) filled with Spanish tortilla de patatas (egg and potatoes).

If you stay around this plaza, you will see that everything happens there: children playing and riding scooters, teenagers getting together for a chat, and the elderly chatting with their friends, smoking cigarettes, feeding the doves, sitting in the coffee shop while having an espresso, reading newspapers, or chatting with friends for hours.

In the heart of Plaza de España y Carrier Sant Miguel, you will find the famous Mercat del Olivar. You can enter this market from all around the building. Here, you can find the best the land and sea can offer: fresh produce, the best quality and variety of meat and charcuterie, exquisite cheeses, the best and freshest seafood, Spanish spices, pickles, and condiments, and wines and dried fruits from the region.

You cannot deny yourself the opportunity to be delighted and indulged with the best of the Majorcan gastronomy: prepared exquisite food; fresh oysters, sushi, cavas, champagne, wines, and liqueurs. It would be a punishment not to try them. In this market, do not miss trying the bars and their famous Spanish tapas, restaurants, and coffee shops, which has one of the best coffees I tried in all my trips.

Also, there is a space in the market where some events can take place. Moreover, you can find beautiful flowers shops, newspapers, stores, and a supermarket to finish your shopping. The market is open from Monday to Friday, from 7:00 a.m. to 2:30 p.m., and on Saturday from 7:00 a.m. to 3:00 p.m. You can indulge in gastronomy from Monday to Saturday until 2:00 p.m. As Plaza de España is the center of Mallorca, it's reasonable to say that this point in town is the entry and exit point. It's where all the streets converge and take you to all the famous stores, businesses, pharmacies, bars, restaurants, coffee shops, and places for Tapeos, and you can find places for entertainment and tour guides.

In front of Plaza de España and next to the train station, you will see another special station that will take you to the enchanted and picturesque town of Soller.

The beautiful and different train that takes you to Soller is a wooden centenary train, which has been working since 1912. It takes one hour to arrive in the Port to Soller. Along the way, you will enjoy the beautiful scenery offered by the Sierra Tremontana.

Arriving in Soller, you will be amazed by the picturesque town. Enjoy the cathedral and walk the very narrow stone paved streets, where you can delight your palate trying authentic gastronomy and shops. From Soller, take the troller train to go to the Port of Soller. This troller passes every thirty minutes, and you will have to buy tickets to get on the train.

In the Port of Soller, you can enjoy the Pueblo de Pescadores, which is one of the port most beautiful on the whole island. In Pueblo de Pescadores, walk around the street along the sea, find souvenirs, and then take the boat to Sa Calobra, which is a in fascinating place along the coastline, full of magical cliffs and caves.

There's an interesting site located in the center of Palma that nobody should miss: the cathedral of Palma. This sandstone, ecclesiastic, magnificent arquitectonic piece of art is famous for the contributions of Antoni Gaudi and Miguel Barcelo.

This breathtaking cathedral makes you wonder how this marvelous place could be built during the reign of Jaime II, around the fourteenth century, using a supreme human imagination to creatre this exquisite gift.

The Royal Palace of the Almudeina, from the fourteenth century, was the official residence of the Spanish Royal Family when they were visiting the island. This Roman castle is a modification of the Muslin Alcazar, and it was the destination for the prosperous Mallorcan Kingdom of the fourteenth century. It can't be missed.

The Plaza Mayor is an inevitable place to visit when in Palma. This Plaza (square) is a perfect longitudinal square, and it was the seat of the Inquisition until 1838. Many wonderful things happen in this gorgeous place: bars, shops, restaurants, food markets, street vendors, coffee shops, events, concerts, dancing, holiday parades, galleries, businesses, and residential apartments. La Plaza Mayor connects you to La Plaza del Court, in which you will see the beautiful and elaborate façade of the Ayuntamiento de Palma, and enjoy the fascinating natural world, the Antiguan Olive tree, which is 600 years old. A pleasurable stroll around the historic city, better called the old city of Palma, is mandatory. It is a picturesque, historic part of the city where you really do not need a map just walking around between its medieval and narrow streets. There you will find the jewels of the Museum of Contemporary Art, the Es Baluard, showing conceptual art, the cathedral, the palace of the Almudaina, gothic churches, and beautiful Catalan authentic houses with exquisite interiors. If you are one of those who enjoys antique literature and treasures, here, I assure you, you will find fascinating antique libraries. If you're of the mind to move to an exciting new place to live, in the old city, you will see all sorts of real estate companies designed to find you your dream home in Mallorca.

The old city connects you with the Passeig del Born, which connects you with the Avenida de Jaime III. In this place, surround yourself with the best and more familiar designers' shops and the most luxury in the world. What's more, find the best gourmet five-star restaurants serving exquisite, tasteful three course meals in style. Also, find the best places to enjoy the most succulent, tasteful, and imaginative Tapas.

The center of Palma is a place full of culture, history, and gastronomy. I also recommend walking around La Rambla Boulevard. La Rambla is an elegant and beautiful place to walk and enjoy its paved avenue, which is designed for pedestrians. In this boulevard, you can find flower shops, restaurants, and coffee shops. If you want to celebrate something special and memorable, or if you just want to experience the best of Palma's fine and exquisite gastronomy, closed by, you will find some hidden gems, like the trendy Toque de Queda and Marc Fonch, which are very famous restaurants located less than three minutes away.

In Palma, you also will enjoy gorgeous, paradise-like beaches, with their crystal-clear blue waters and white powder sands. The beaches are located along the coasts of Palma in the Mediterranean Sea. I recommend some of the ones I had the pleasure to visit: Cala Gamba, Cala Major, Platja Cala Guix, Platja d'Illetes, Platja d'Or, Playa de Palma, Platja Cala Estancia, Playa Ciudad de Jardín, Cala Nova, Platja Buguenvl-lia, Playa S'Arenal, and Platja Cas Catala Calvia. You can visit these beaches by using public transportation, renting a boat, rental cars, or renting scooters.

When visiting Palma, while you enjoy its beaches, do not fail to visit its majestic castles, such as Castillo de Alvaro, which is the most beautiful castle of Mallorca and dates from around the year 902. There's also the Castillo de Santueri. the Castillo de Bellver. This last castle is situated in Palma, and has a Mallorcan Gothic style. It was built at the top of a hill surrounded by thick vegetation.

Palma de Mallorca, Spain

Cathedral Santa Maria de Mallorca
Palma de Mallorca, Spain

Aerial Views: Palma de Mallorca Coast, Spain

Cala Major Palma

Palacio de la Almudeina.
Interior View

Soller, Palma de Mallorca

Palma de Mallorca, Spain

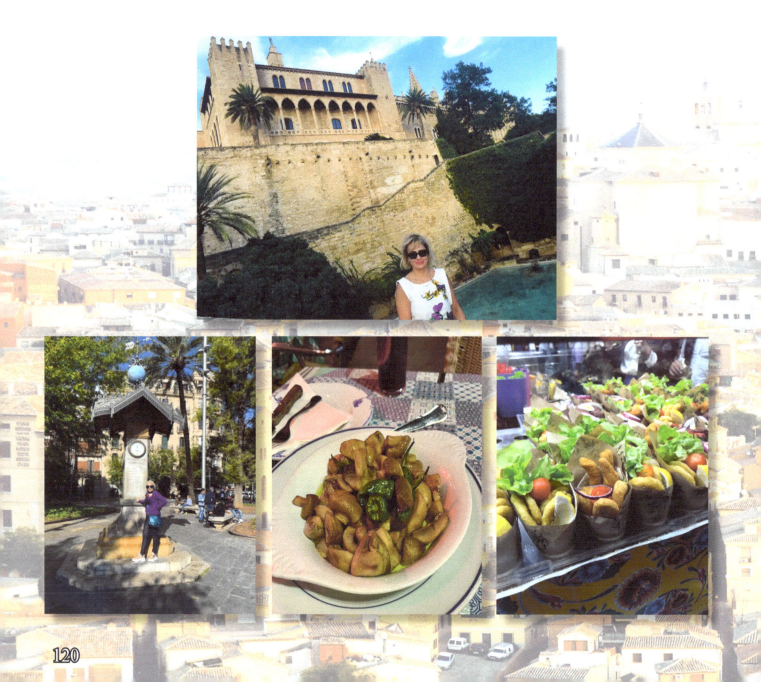

Palma de Mallorca, Spain

Shrimps in Olive Oil and Garlic **Tarta Al Whisky**

Palma de Mallorca, Spain

Palma de Mallorca, Spain

Palma de Mallorca, Spain

SPANISH RECIPES

Andalusian Gazpacho

3 ½ oz. French bread, crust removed
2 lbs. very ripe tomatoes peeled
1 green bell pepper chopped
2 cloves garlic, peeled
¼ cup white wine vinegar
2/3 cup olive oil
2 Tsp. salt

Garnish:
1 small onion.
1 firm, ripe tomato, peeled & chopped.
1 green bell pepper, chopped.
2 oz. cucumber, peeled & chopped
1 egg, hardboiled, chopped.
3 ½ oz. French bread, diced.

Note: All chopped items should be finely chopped.

Directions:

Soak bread in 2 cups of water for a few minutes until soggy. Remove the crust and squeeze out until dry. In a food processor, purée the garlic, tomatoes, bread, and salt, then add oil gradually, followed by vinegar. Season at the end. Refrigerate. Garnish and serve chilled.

Breaded Baked Tomatoes

2 Large, ripe tomatoes
2 Tbsp. olive oil
4 Tbsp. breadcrumbs
2 Tbsp. fresh parsley leaves, chopped.
Salt and pepper to taste

Directions:

Preheat oven 350°F. Cut tomatoes in half. Drizzle each part with olive oil. Sprinkle with salt, pepper, and parsley leaves. Cover each part with breadcrumbs. Bake tomatoes for about 20-25 minutes or until golden brown on top.

Chilled Almond & Garlic Soup

1 ½ cups almonds
5 oz. French bread, crust removed.
2 garlic cloves, peeled
2/3 cup olive oil
1 Tbsp. sherry vinegar
4 cups cold water
1 lb. Muscat grapes, peeled and seeded (garnish)
Dash of salt

Directions:

Soak bread in a small amount of water. In a food processor, crush the almonds, bread, garlic, and salt. Gradually drizzle the mixture with olive oil, forming a spongy paste. Mix in vinegar, then add cold water. Refrigerate.

Before serving, check the salt and vinegar. Garnish with grapes and serve well chilled.

Cold Watermelon Salad

1 medium watermelon, diced in large pieces
1 cup feta cheese.
1 cucumber, sliced
½ red onion
2 Tbsp. lemon juice Salt
Pepper
Cilantro (garnish)

Directions:

Place watermelon in the refrigerator for an hour. Arrange watermelon, cucumber, feta cheese and red onion and sprinkle with lemon juice, salt, and pepper. Garnish with cilantro. Serve chilled immediately.

Crema Catalana (Catalan Custard)

½ cup cornstarch
1 stick cinnamon
6 egg yolks
4 cups milk
lemon zest
1 ¼ cups sugar

Directions:

Dissolve cornstarch in a cup of milk. Heat remaining milk with the stick of cinnamon and lemon zest. Bring to a boil. Meanwhile, blend egg yolks with a cup of sugar. Strain boiled milk through a fine sieve, then pour over egg mixture. Add the dissolved cornstarch, mix well, and heat again, stirring constantly in one direction. Do not allow the boiling mixture to separate.

When it thickens, remove from heat and transfer to a serving dish or individual bowls. When the mixture cools, sprinkle the top with sugar and immediately, over an open flame, caramelize the sugar until it forms a firm, thin caramel layer.

Ensalada De Frutas (Fruit Salad)

1 watermelon, diced.
2 mangos, diced.
1 cup strawberries, diced.
1 cantaloupe, diced.

Directions:

Scoop out watermelon with a spoon, and cut the edges as shown in photo. Dice mangos and cantaloupe into ½" cubes. Mix all fruits in a bowl and place them inside the watermelon. Serve chilled.

Ensalada Mixta (Mixed Salad)

2 onions
2 Kirby cucumbers, peeled.
2 eggs, hardboiled
1 small can tuna
¼ olive oil
2 Tbsp. white wine vinegar
Salt

Directions:

Dice all ingredients into finely cut, ½" cubes. Dress with olive oil, vinegar, and salt. Chill for at least an hour before serving.

Grilled Eggplant & Red Peppers

1 eggplant
1 red bell pepper
2 Tbsp. olive oil
2 Tbsp. parsley leaves, chopped.
Salt and pepper to taste

Directions:

Slice eggplant and set aside skin. Cut the pepper ¼-inch thick lengthwise and set aside. Grill the eggplant and pepper on a stove grill until brown outside. Place in a serving dish. Drizzle with olive oil and sprinkle salt and pepper.

Toss and serve.

Grouper In Matelote Sauce

2 lbs. thick grouper fillets
1/3 cup olive oil (plus more for frying)
6 ½ oz. onion, finely chopped
10 oz. ripe tomatoes, peeled and finely chopped.
1 Tbsp. parsley (garnish)
3 cloves garlic, peeled
1/3 cup olive oil (plus more for frying)
1 cup almonds, toasted
2 Tbsp. hazelnuts, toasted
1 thick slice French bread, fried.
½ cup water
¼ cup dry white wine
Dash of salt

Directions:

Heat oil and sauté onions. When brownish, add tomatoes and fry until it forms a thick mixture. Add parsley and paprika and remove from heat. In a mortar, crush garlic, almond, hazelnuts, and fried bread. Add tomato mixture and stir to blend. Add water and wine and continue stirring. Pour the mixture in a shallow casserole dish and cook for about 10 minutes. Place fish slices on top of tomato sauce, season with salt, and cover. Cook on low heat for 8 minutes. Garnish with parsley and serve.

Seafood Paella

Broth:
8 oz. monkfish
1 hake or other fish head
8 oz. small sea crayfish or shrimp (prawns)
1/3 cup olive oil
1 medium onion, chopped
1 medium tomato, peeled & finely chopped.
1 tsp. paprika
8 cups water Salt to taste
All-purpose flour (for coating)

Rice:
1 lb. mussels
4 medium shrimp (prawns)
8 oz. squid chopped
2 pinches of saffron.
1/3 cup olive oil
1 medium tomato peeled & finely chopped.
1 tsp. paprika
2 ½ cups medium grain rice

Directions:

Broth: Coat monkfish and hake with flour. Heat oil in a casserole dish, fry shrimp, then remove and set aside. Fry monkfish and hake head in the same oil, then remove and set aside. Sauté onion until brown, then add tomato and fry for a few minutes. Add paprika, then water and a little salt and continue cooking. Meanwhile, remove the skin and bones from the fried fish. Add these scraps to the broth and set the fish aside. Peel shrimp and set aside. Crush the heads, shells, and legs in a mortar and add to broth. Cover the casserole and cook broth over medium heat for about 45 minutes, then strain through a fine sieve.

Rice: Steam mussels. Remove empty shell halves and set aside. Strain the liquid produced and add to the broth. Add a little salt to shrimp. Heat up fish broth and add saffron. Heat oil on a 16-inch paella pan, add garlic and tomato, and gently fry shrimp and squid for a few minutes. Add paprika and rice. Stir and add 5 ½ cups of fish broth. Check the seasoning. Cook for 10 minutes.

Add fish and shrimp tails, lower the heat, and cook for another 8-10 minutes. Taste the rice to check if done. Remove from heat. Arrange mussels decoratively on top. Let stand for 5 minutes and serve.

Tortillas de Patatas (Potato Omelet)

1 ½ lbs. potatoes
1 1/3 cups olive oil
Salt
6 eggs
1 large onion

Directions:

In a medium bowl, beat eggs and set aside. In a medium skillet, heat oil over medium-high heat and sauté onion until brown. Add potatoes and cook until tender. Add salt and eggs and cook until eggs are done and tortilla becomes easy to flip. Transfer to a serving dish. Tortilla can be served hot or at room temperature.

CHAPTER VIII

A Trip to France

From Barcelona Sant Railway station to Bordeaux St Jean Train Station France

There are at least eight daily trains from Barcelona to Bordeaux, France. The earlier in advance you book the tickets, the cheaper the tickets become, so I advise you to plan and book the tickets between three to six months in advance. This way you will get the best fares and best trip. The fastest train from Barcelona to Bordeaux, France takes six hours and fifty-five minutes with two stops.

Bordeaux is situated in the southwest of France, and it is the major port of the Garrone River. Bordeaux is the fifth largest city in France after Paris. It was designated by UNESCO as a world heritage site in 2007 due to its outstanding architectural ensemble, seen between preserved buildings and history. Bordeaux offers riverside walks, skiing, surfing, history, and lot of culture and local gastronomy, all in a relatively small city.

Bordeaux is the world wine capital, and its wine production dates back to the eighth century. The wine industry is its major economy, along with food processing, light engineering, the manufacturing of textiles, clothing, chemicals, the production of aerospace equipment, car components, and electronics.

Since 1945, Bordeaux has continued to expand, adding new suburbs and small towns. What was once the surrounding areas has nowadays been incorporated into the city. The population, as well as commercial activities, has shifted from the center of the city to the peripherals.

The southwest of France has preserved its traditions, and is seen in history itself in the golden stone villages of the region, where the elderly wear the barest clothing and walk with canes; they sit in their armchairs beside the fire and shell chestnuts and walnuts, while Frenchmen of all ages play boules in the parks or squares. Boules is without a doubt France's most popular game. The aim is to toss a heavy metal ball as close as possible to a small central ball.

Walking by the modern city of Bordeaux is an exquisite enchantment. It has perfect weather combined with history, which you can see for yourself when you're surrounded by a semicircle of boulevards, where beyond lie the suburbs of Le Bouscat, Cauderan, Merignac, Talence, and Begles. The Garrone River separates the city from the suburb of La Bastide. Along the river, you can see broad quays, with tall warehouses behind, factories, and breathtaking mansions. Some gates of the old city walls remain, as well as ruins from the Roman amphitheater and The Grand Theatre. Further along the quay is the Esplanade des Quincoces, one of the largest squares in Europe. Some main ecclesiastical sites in Bordeaux that cannot be missed during your visit are Saint Andre Cathedral and the Saint Michel Tower from the fifteenth century.

Discovering markets in Bordeaux was my favorite excitement and pleasure due to their numbers and variety. The cornerstone of each good French village is its markets. There are several bustling markets around Bordeaux, which are all worth a visit. The most famous and biggest of them is the Marche de Capucins, on the Cours de la Marne. This market opens every day except Mondays. It is an open-air place that you can find most fresh meat, fish, cheeses, charcuterie, vegetables, spices, local wines, plus places to eat, small bars, and taverns where you can taste the regional tidbits and cafés. The market is beautiful, but it's not very clean and can be smelly.

The Cap Ferret Market is located in the small town of the same name. It is open daily in the summer; otherwise, it's only open on Wednesdays and Saturdays. This is a brilliant market that sells fresh produce, crafts, and a vast array of unusual items.

Then there's Marche Hebdomadaire in Le Porge. This market opens weekly, and it's located in the coastal town of Le Porge, west of Bordeaux. In this market you can find fresh produce, local farmers, and homemade arts and crafts.

Marche de Soulac is next. This market is situated in the Soulac-sur-Mer. It opens every morning and during some evenings during July and August. In these markets during the beautiful summer months, there's a Gourmet Fair where dozens of traditional exhibitors with local delicacies are on display, allowing the visitors to enjoy their wines, spirits, liquors, Foie Gras, and charcuterie, as well as some other regional products.

Then there's Place de la Republique. This market is held on Sunday morning on the ground floor of Hotel de France, and local products as well as artisans are displayed.

It's beautiful and entertaining to spend the night under the starts during the summer, wandering this paradisal city, that besides everything else, offers great night entertainment for the whole family, as well as music. You can find tables where you can sit and enjoy it in a relaxed atmosphere with food and drinks.

Bordeaux represents the best living conditions in France. Due to its affordable housing compared to the French capital and to the job markets, Les Bordelais eat in style, and they for sure know how to use traditional ingredients that bring the aroma of the whole region to the tastebuds, such as stuffed goose neck, preserved goose and duck confit, foie gras, and truffles.

They are experts in preserving meats by cooking them slowly and lovingly in their own fat, then storing them in earthenware pots. When it comes to shellfish, the region has outstanding mussels, oysters, shrimps, crabs, cockles, clams, whelks, scallops and a lot more. Bordeaux's most celebrated dish is entrecôte marchand de vin, also known as entrecôte à la bordelaise, which is a dish of rib steak cooked in a rich gravy made from Bordeaux wine, butter, shallots, herbs, and bone marrow. Certainly, these dishes go well with a hearty Bordeaux red. Boeuf de Bazas is beef raised near Bazas. You can also enjoy excellent hams and succulent lambs, such as as Agneau de Pauillac. This is a dish of lamb raised on the salt marshes round Pouillac, and is often served with truffles. Then there's mijote d'agneau aux mojettes, which is lamb meat cooked with white beans.

You can also get a crusted rack of young goat with bordelaise sauce. L'egouttoir recouvert de jeune chèvre avec la sauce bordelaise is a succulent rack of goat served on a bed of scalloped potatoes with a bordelaise sauce. Maquereau avec les poireaux Rochelle is perfectly cooked mackerel, balancing its flavor with leeks and Dijon mustard.

Snails are popular, and are often served in a casserole with Bordeaux wine, tomatoes, and Cognac. Soupe aux moules is a creamy, rich mussel soup, loaded with mussels, saffron, and cream and served with garlic chilli bread. Then there's's escargot avec le beurre d'ail snails. This is plum snails fed on grape leaves and served in garlic butter with a dash of crème fraîche on toast. Figs avec le jambon poitou et le fromage de chèvres is a class act of ripe, luscious figs straight from the tree, with goat cheese and Poitou ham. Sweet treats include cannelés, caramelised brioche-style pastries, or the famous marrons glaces, which are candied chestnuts, or noisettines du medoc, roasted hazelnuts rolled in sugar.

Reflections on the Water, Place de la Bourse, Bordeaux, France

Castle on Hill Overlooking Vineyards with Rows of Grapes on a Clear Summer Day, Bordeaux, France

Paris

Paris is the exquisite, magnificent, many-hued city, the so-called "city of lights," because wherever or whatever you look at is impregnated with all sorts of artistic forms from history: sculptures, symphonic music, fashion, architectural interior design, theater, literature, poetry, paintings, drawings, and you cannot miss the art culinaire. The cuisine in France is intended to please the eyes more that the tongue. There is no doubt that the Parisian chefs know the subtle, perfect, impeccable style of balancing the finest ingredients, creating dishes that will become part of a daily masterpiece of art, and they serve them with absolutely elegance.

Wandering the streets of Paris, one sees narrow cobblestone streets with lanterns decorating the sides, as if it were a painting by Van Gogh, and the ringing bells of the churches echo in the background. Restaurants and cafés line the sides of the streets, with tables outside where you can sit and taste the perfection of the local dishes with a robust red. Paris is the city where we can let our imaginations fly, where meeting the maestros from the Golden Age in Mont Martre seems possible. Mont Martre, the highest point in the city of Paris, is where all the artists and creative minds from all over the world gather to discuss and argue—with a glass of wine or dinner. It is a place where we can all enjoy a conversation of how we can better enjoy Paris, or even better, how to help reshape the world.

There are no better places to enjoy Paris and the Parisians than with a romantic walk under the rain through the colorful trees and flowers of Les Champs Elysées and the Arc de Thomphe. You can enjoy the cultural, foggy old streets of Paris, where you can find fine antiques, music, vinyl records, and old books. Then there are architectural treasures like Museum de Louvre, The Eiffel Tower, and Norte Dame Cathedral, or once can walk toward La place de la Concorde to enjoy its most famous fountains. Take a trip in the riverboat through the calm, beautiful waters of the Seine, sightseeing Paris at night, where you can see in the distance the illuminated Opéra Garnier. Visitors walk in the rain over its romantic bridges, become engaged in this city, or travel back in time to visit the majestic Versailles palace.

Paris is the only city in the world that permits us to rediscover all of our senses. All becomes art. This city reminds us that pleasure runs everything. Paris inspires us to fall in love, and when we understand that every single thing we do is passion, then making love is solely intended to help us lose our fear of death. We realize we are for sure loving, and all we are experiencing is a divine souvenir of life.

In France, every road leads to splendid food, and the French live to eat. The French gastronomy was created accordingly with its climate. A stroll along narrow country lanes, or a ramble through the woods by forests paths, yields the reward of armfuls of perfumes, the scents of fresh grass, thousands of aromas, and then its cuisine.

The variety of landscape creates a variety in its cuisine. Nowhere else in the whole world we can find arid deserts, luxurious gardens, golden beaches shaded by palm trees, and vast landscape that remain untouched, where the horizon gets lost in the infinite in a relatively short distance. These lands provide us with their finest ingredients, which will produce thousands of good recipes. Without this, France would not be France.

Each province in France is a piece of the puzzle, because throughout history, each region has maintained its originality and its culinary traditions. Beer and charcuterie predominate eastern France, the south is known for fresh vegetables cooked al dente and garden herbs, and the use of butter cuisine is heavier in frigid northern regions. In contrast, the use of cuisine oils are lighter in the south of France. From mountain to mountain, the milk pastures and the local cheeses are produced, and lambs and sheep are fed free range.

From Paris I went to the Southeastern Provence Region by Bus

This is a picturesque region where sea, hills, and mountains fuse together. The Alpes-Maritimes is formed by Cannes—famous for its film festival—Nice, Saint-Tropez, and Monaco. The region is better known as Le côté d'azur in French. Traveling through Provence is lovely, with its flowery lavender fields along the coast, the perfume of rose petals lingering in the air from distilleries in Var. This hilly country is somewhat secluded, but lights up when we begin climbing around the many villages. It is here between this rocky cliff that the kitchen-garden cuisine originated. The families, their recipes, and their techniques created an independent cooking style that has laid its flavors over centuries. In Provence, cooking is an artist's affair. There is neither too much shadow nor too much sun, neither excessive colors nor dominant flavors that shape this eloquent culinary treasure. This character is reflected in thick soups: fish soups, crab soups, tomato soup, fava bean soup, squash soup, or green bean soup. There's great classic aioli, cream salt cod, brandade de morue, or pan bagnat, whose classic niçoise ingredients are tomatoes, olives, sweet peppers, and young broad beans. The provinces eat their snack or merenda—as said in niçoise dialect, which is rooted in the Italian language—with French bread rubbed with garlic, tapenade, anchoïade, or bonnes pâtes, which is made from chickpea flour. Famous chefs have taken advantage of the niçoise cuisine to bring "fashionable" and "delicious" back to country food.

Some connoisseurs used to call this Provençal cuisine "Cuisine of the Poor," because in the French Alpes-Maritimes, it is said the cooking is neither the worst Italian cooking nor the best niçoise-Italian. I say this because of the proximity of this region to the Italian coast.

The Provençal cuisine is a more Mediterranean cuisine, with vegetables, figs, some goat's milk products, anchovies, black olives, and chickpeas. The famous socca, which is a large flat cake made of fava beans, is cooked in a hot wood-fired oven. This region also produce lavender honey and almond nougat, so you can imagine the smell when traveling the Provençal roads. This region breeds the best lambs in the world, and produces the famous Banon cheeses, which are made from goat's milk. They also harvest wild mushrooms and truffles. In Provence, it is a sin to miss a subtle red or wonderfully fine white wine from the famous chateau de Crémât, château de Bellet, or when visiting their precious vineyards while indulging in good food.

The region embraces influences from Piedmont and the Ligurian coast in Italy, so ravioli, gnocchi, capellini, and tortellini are part of the local culinary history.

The provinces have their distinctive moods and personalities, which have been seen, captured, and reflected in many works of art by famous writers, poets, and painters, such as Picasso, Van Gogh, Matisse, and others.

The French Riviera, with Nice, Saint-Tropez, and Monaco, is a favorite resort vacation destination of aristocrats, famous artists, and wealthy families from around the world. It's well known for its beautiful modern hotels, casinos, paradisal beaches, and marinas, like the Promenade des Anglais in Nice, or Monte Carlo Casino in Monaco. Every year, this region hosts fifty percent of the super-yacht fleets from around the world. The beautiful French coastline is very small, and it can be toured in a couple of days.

Paris Skyline

Storefront Desserts, Paris

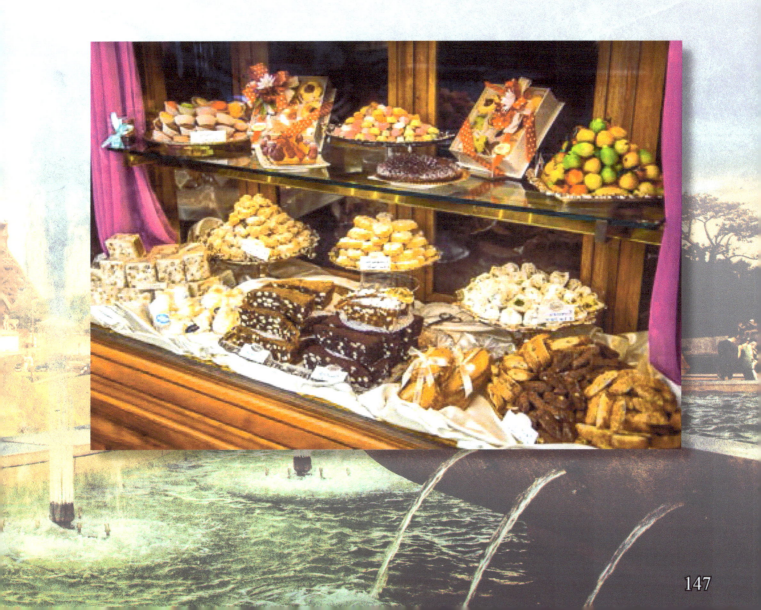

French Recipes

Caramelized Onion Tart

For the pastry:
1 1/3 cups all purpose flour
1/4 Tsp. salt
1/2 cup very cold unsalted butter
1/4 cup ice water
2 Tbsp. Dijon mustard
1/4 cup of shredded Gruyère cheese
2 large eggs
1/3 cup heavy cream
1 1/2 Tsp. fresh thyme

Caramelized onion:
6 large onions   1 Tbsp. unsalted butter
1/4 cup olive oil   1 Tsp. of sugar
1/2 Tsp. salt   Sprinkles of freshly ground pepper

Directions:

To make the pastry, combine the flour and salt in a food processor. Pulse for a few seconds to blend. Add the butter and process until the mixture resembles coarse meal, about 5-10 seconds. With the motor running, add the ice water and process until the dough comes together. Add when pinched. Transfer the dough to a floured work surface and bring together into a rough mass. Press into a rectangular shape and roll out into a rectangle large enough to fit an 11x8-inch tart pan with removable bottom. Alternatively, press the dough into a round disk and roll out into a circle large enough to fit an 11-inch round tart pan with removable bottom. Drape the dough over the rolling pin and position it over the pan. Unroll the dough and ease it into the pan, pressing it against the sides and bottom without stretching. Trim the excess dough by gently running the rolling pin across the top of the pan. Prick the dough with a fork and refrigerate until firm, about 30 minutes.

Preheat the oven to 375°F. Place the tart pan on a baking sheet. Line the dough with parchment baking paper and fill with pie weights, raw rice, or dried beans. Bake until very light brown, 20-25 minutes. Let cool completely on a wire rack and remove weights and paper. Brush the shell with the mustard and sprinkle with 2 tbs of the cheese. Return to the oven and bake until the cheese is melted, about 7 minutes. Let cool completely. Reduce the oven temperature to 350°F.

In a bowl, beat together the eggs, cream, thyme, and 1/2 cup of cheese. Add the caramelized onions and stir to combine. Spoon into the tart shell and sprinkle with the remaining cheese. Bake until cheese is melted, and filling is set, 30-35 minutes. Let cool. Remove the sides of the pan and transfer the tart to a serving plate. Serve warm or room temperature.

Caramelized onions

Melt 1/2 unsalted butter in a fry pan with 1/4 cup of olive oil. Add the onions, 1 teaspoon of sugar, 1/2 teaspoon of salt, and ground pepper and cook in a slow heat, stirring often until onions are brown.

Omelette Quercynoise

10 eggs
Salt and ground Pepper
2 Tsp. of brandy
12 walnuts coarsely grated.
4 oz of Roquefort cheese
1 Tbsp. of goose fat

Directions:

Break the eggs into a bowl and beat with a fork until blended, adding salt, pepper, and brandy. Mix the walnuts and crumble the Roquefort.

Melt the goose fat in a non-stick 10-inch skillet. Pour in the egg mixture and cook the omelet over low heat, delicately stirring the surface, until it's firm on the bottom. Turn it over the skillet until the other side is cooked. Slide the omelet onto a plate and serve immediately.

French Pumpkin Soup

2 lbs. pumpkin peeled & seeded
2 Tbsp. olive oil.
2 celery stalks trimmed & sliced
1 garlic clove.
1 onion
4 aromatic cloves
1 carrot sliced
3 ¾ cups chicken stock.
Crème fraiche (garnish)

Directions:

In a medium skillet, over medium-high heat, sauté onions and garlic until brown. Add garlic clove and cook until fragrance is released. Add carrots and celery and sauté until slightly brown. Add pumpkin and cook until slightly brown. Reduce heat and transfer to a pot. Add chicken stock and simmer 45-60 minutes, until vegetables are tender. Blend the soup in a blender in small batches. Serve hot in individual bowls, adding a spoon of crème fraîche on top for garnish.

French Carrot Salad with Lemon Dijon

- 1 lb. cooked carrots, peeled & sliced ½" thick
- 2 Tbsp. Dijon mustard.
- 1 Tbsp. fresh-squeezed lemon juice
- 1 ½ Tbsp. vegetable oil
- 1-2 Tbsp. honey
- Salt and pepper to taste
- 2 Tbsp. fresh parsley leaves, chopped
- 2 scallions, finely chopped.

Directions:

In a medium bowl, combine Dijon mustard, parsley, scallions, oil, honey, lemon juice, salt and pepper. Add to the carrots and toss well. Serve chilled.

Endive Red Apple Salad

2 shallots or red onions, julienne-cut
2 Tbsp. white wine vinegar
2 Tbsp. red wine vinegar
1 Tbsp. olive oil
1 Tbsp. walnut oil
4 cups Red Delicious apples, julienne-cut
3 heads Belgium endives, sliced lengthwise
2 Tbsp. parsley leaves, chopped.

Directions:

Combine oils with vinegar, salt, and pepper. Combine endive, apples, and parsley in a large bowl. Toss to coat. Serve chilled immediately.

Carbonnade Belgium Beef & Beer Stew

- 2 ½ lbs. boneless chuck roast, trimmed and cut into ½" cubes
- 5 cups cremini mushrooms
- 3 Tbsp. all-purpose flour
- 2 cups carrots, cut in ½"-thick slices
- 2 Tbsp. Dijon mustard
- 1 Tsp. fresh thyme
- 1 bay leaf
- 2 cups onions, chopped.
- 2 garlic cloves, minced.
- 12 oz. bottle of Belgian amber beer
- 1 ¾ cup parsnips, cut in ½"-thick slices.
- Salt and pepper to taste
- ½ Tsp. caraway seeds

Directions:

In a large skillet, over medium-high heat, sauté onions and garlic until brown. Add mushrooms and cook for 6 minutes, then add bay leaf, thyme, caraway seeds, salt, and pepper. Cook until fragrant. Add meat and cook until brown. Add carrots, parsnips, and Dijon mustard, and cook for 5 more minutes. Transfer to a slow crock pot. Pour in the amber beer and beef cubes. Stir well and leave to cook overnight in low heat. Serve hot.

Pommel De Terre Au Gratin (Potato Gratin)

2 lbs. potatoes peeled and cut in slices 1/3 in thick boiling broth or water as needed.
Salt
1/2 cup Gruyère cheese or Parmesan grated or a mixture of both.
1/2 cup whipping cream.
2 eggs
Whole nutmeg

Directions:

Preheat oven 350°F. Put the potatoes in a saucepan and pour just enough boiling broth to cover. Season with salt if using water. Cover and simmer until the potatoes are nearly done, about 15 minutes. Remove from the heat.

Combine half of the cheese, cream, and eggs in a bowl. Scrape in a bit of the nutmeg and whisk together until well blended. Pour the mixture into the potatoes, swirl the content of the saucepan, and then pour them into a gratin dish. Smooth the surface and sprinkle the remaining cheese. Place in the oven and bake until the surface is golden and the potatoes are set in a light custard, about 20 minutes. Serve immediately.

Papeton D'aubergines (Molded Eggplant Pudding)

3 lbs eggplants
Salt
Olive oil as needed.
5 eggs
1 cup of milk
1 Tsp. of saffron dissolved in 1 Tbsp. of boiling water
3 cups of tomato sauce, heated.

Directions:

Cut off the stem ends from the eggplants. Slice 2 or 3 lengthwise slices 1/3-inch thick from the center to over the sides. Salt the slices and sides and leave in a colander to drain for 39 minutes. Sponge dry with paper towels. Preheat oven to 350°F. In a large frying pan, pour in the olive oil to a depth of 1/4-inch and place over medium heat. Slip the eggplant slices, a few at a time, into the hot oil and fry, turning once, until golden on both sides, about 10 minutes. Add more oil as needed. Place on paper towels to drain. Then fry the cross hatched sides in the same manner and drain on paper towels. Scrape all the flesh from the cross hatched sides into a bowl and mash to a purée with fork. Add the eggs and pinch of salt and whisk together. Then work in the milk and dissolve saffron until thoroughly incorporated. Set aside. Line up a 6-cup circular savarin mold with a well with the eggplant slices, overlapping them slightly and pressing firmly into place. The tips should extend beyond the outer rim and the central well. Pour in the custard mixture and fold the extending tips over the surface.

Place the mold in a large oven pan and pour in boiling water to reach halfway up the sides to form a bain-marie. Place in the oven and bake until the surface of the custard is no longer liquid, about 40 minutes. Remove from Bain-Marie and leave to settle for 10 minutes. To unmold, fold a kitchen towel lengthwise and place the mold on it. Place an overturned platter on top and grip the ridge of the mold, protected by the towel, using your fingernails. While holding the platter firmly in place with your thumbs, turn over the mold and platter together. Lift off the mold. Pour a ribbon of tomato sauce around the outside of the papeton and pour the remainder into a heated bowl to serve alongside.

Anchoiade Anchovy Spread

12 anchovies preserved in salt.
6 fresh cloves of garlic
3 fresh shallots
1 Tbsp. of red wine vinegar
3/4 cup of extra virgin olive oil
6 spring parsley finely chopped.
French baguette toasted.
Raw vegetables: cauliflower, radish, fennel, artichokes, peppers, celery

Directions:

Rinse the anchovies under cold running water and rub them to remove all traces of salt. Combine the chopped anchovies, garlic, and shallots in a food processor. Add the vinegar and blend until smooth. With the machine running, pour the olive oil in a thin stream, then add the parsley and blend for 10 seconds. Serve the spread as a dip with French bread and raw vegetables.

Cervelle De Canut (Herbed Cheese Spread)

This is a dish traditionally served in mâchons, the bistros of Lyon. The name refers to a small meal that was eaten in the mid-morning.

8 oz fresh fromage Blanca or ricotta cheese
1/4 cup of olive oil
3 Tbsp. white wine vinegar
3 Tbsp. dry white wine
3/4 cup chilled cream
2 French shallots finely chopped.
2 spring flat leaf parsley leaves only and finely chopped.
6 spring chervil finely chopped.
10 chives stalk finely chopped.
Salt and pepper to taste

Directions:

Set the cheese to drain in a colander for 12 hours before preparation. Turn the drained cheese into a bowl and mash with a fork. Mix in the oil, vinegar and wine.

Whip the cream until stiff and fold into cheese mixture. Mix in the shallots, herbs, salt and pepper. Chill thoroughly. Serve the cheese with whole grain country bread or rye bread.

FRENCH DESSERT

Gâteau Basque (Basque Cake)

4 1/2 oz of butter
2 1/4 cup of all-purpose flour
1 Tsp. of rum
1 Tsp. of baking powder
1 Tsp. of vanilla extract
2 pinches of salt
1 Tbsp. of dark rum

For the filling:
1 cup of milk
3 egg yolks
1/3 cup powdered sugar
1/4 cup all-purpose flour
1 Tbsp. of dark rum
1 Tsp. of vanilla

For the glaze:
1 egg yolk
1 Tbsp. of milk

Directions:

Melt the butter in a small saucepan over low heat, then let cool. Combine the eggs, sugar, and vanilla and mix well. Blend in the butter and rum. Sift the flour, baking powder, and salt and stir until soft dough forms. Refrigerate for 1 hour.

Meanwhile, prepare the filling. Bring the milk to simmer in a small saucepan. Combine the egg yolks and sugar in a large saucepan and whisk until pale in color. Mix in the flour. Beat in the hot milk. Place the saucepan over medium heat and cook the custard until it thickens, beating constantly. Let boil for one minute, then remove from heat and add the rum and vanilla. Let cool, stirring occasionally. Preheat oven to 400°F. Butter a 10-inch round pan. Divide the dough into two pieces, one a little larger than the other. Roll out the larger portion into a 9-inch circle 3/8-inch (1 cm) thick. Carefully line the cake pan with the dough, flattening it against the sides. Spread the custard on top and turn the edge of the dough circle back over the custard, but do not press down. Moisten the edge of the dough with a pastry brush dipped in cold water. Roll out the remaining dough into 9-inch circle and lower it into the pan to cover the custard.

For the glaze, beat the egg yolk and milk and brush over the top of the cake. Bake the cake for 40 minutes or until golden brown. Let cool before turning out of the pan. Let the cake rest at room temperature for a few hours before serving.

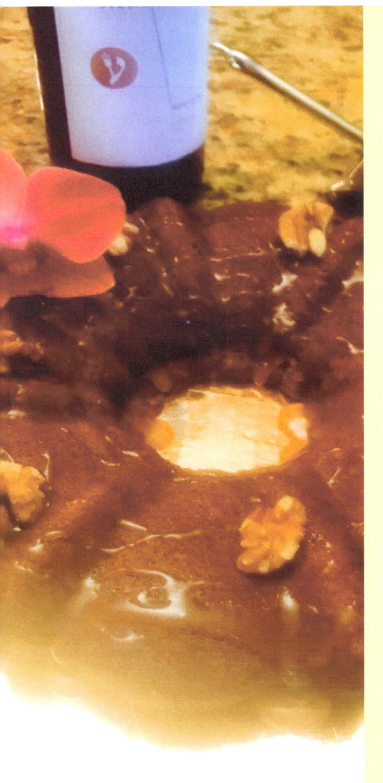

Grenoblois (Grenoble Caramel Walnut Cake)

10 oz butter
3/4 cup of breadcrumbs
1 cup powdered sugar
3 Tbsps. of dark rum
6 eggs separated.
8 oz walnuts
1 Tsp. of coffee extract

For serving:
6 Tbsps. of sugar
6 Tbsps. of water
1/2 Tsp. of fresh lemon juice
Walnuts

Directions:

Preheat oven to 400°F. Butter a 9-inch round cake pan. Melt the butter over low heat in a small saucepan and let cool. Finely chop the walnuts in a food processor. Combine the egg yolks with 2/3 cup of sugar and whisk until the mixture doubles in volume and is pale in color, about 10 minutes. Fold in the butter, rum, and coffee extract, then the breadcrumbs and walnuts.

Beat the egg whites to soft peaks, then gradually add the remaining sugar and beat until smooth and shiny. Gently fold the egg whites into the walnut's mixture. Pour the butter into the prepared pan and bake until browned, about 35 minutes.

Meanwhile, combine the 6 tablespoons of sugar, water, and lemon juice in a small saucepan and bring to boil. Cook until dark caramel forms.

Turn the cake out into a serving plate. Pour the caramel over and decorate with walnuts. Let cool completely before serving.

French Sweet Crepes with Straberry Sauce (Dairy Free Option)

2 Cups of flour
3 Eggs
¼ Cup of butter (melted)
3 Tbsp. sugar
3 Cups of milk (rice or oat milk)
Fresh strawberries for garnishing

Directions

Mix flour and sugar, then add eggs and melted butter (or oil). Add the milk and mix until the batter is smooth. Pour ¼ cup of batter on a heated, flat oily pan and tilt pan to spread evenly into a thin layer. When cooked through (about 2 minutes), flip and cook other side.

Straberry Sauce

8 Strawberries
1/8 Cup sugar
2 Tsp. cornstarch

Directions:

Dice strawberries and place them in a saucepan. Sprinkle sugar on top and turn heat on low. When sugar melts, add cornstarch and stir until hot and bubbly (don't overcook or sauce will harden).

Presentation:

Place fresh strawberries inside crepe, fold, and drizzle sauce on top.

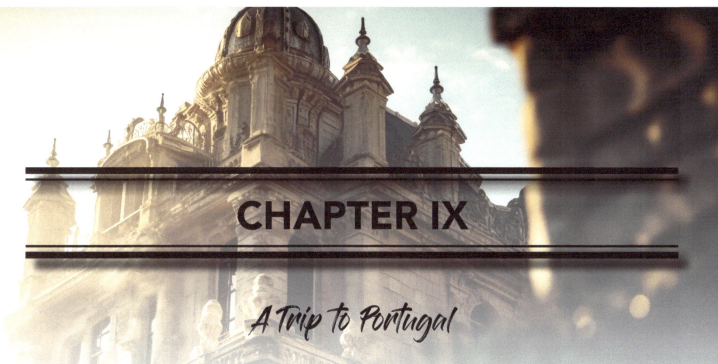

CHAPTER IX

A Trip to Portugal

Portugal is a neighboring country of Spain by way of the Atlantic Ocean. It has a long history of austerity, failed governments, dictatorship, and military coup de état. During the twentieth century, the country revolutionized and became what it is today a: metropolis. Even though Portugal is a little country with around 11 million people, it is a country of grand importance in Europe, because its production of wine and its variety of autochthonous grapes only compares with Italy's, which makes the Portuguese variety of wine one of the more antique flavors in the world, and one of the more delicious. Their most famous is Port wine.

Gastronomically speaking, Portugal doesn't have the variety either in its gastronomy nor in its population compared with Spain. As the connoisseurs of "the art gastronomic," many Spaniards believe that Portugal's dishes are somehow a bit gray, plain, and simple. Although respecting their opinion, I don't agree. By contrast, I think the Portuguese dishes are full of flavors. They are a marvelous surprise, marked with emotions that make our senses get lost.

It's a delightful trying the best: Port wine, the Francesinhas, and its pastelitos the nata. The Portuguese food is somehow hidden in its descriptions.

Lisbon

For a long time, the city of Lisbon has worn a costume in relation to its tourism and what they can offer to adventurous travelers, but Lisbon invites us to discreetly enjoy the past and the present because of its combination of different generations. This intermix gives the city a majestic enchantment of its own. Lisbon offers us an old charm, a rich culture, and breathtaking architecture.

You can discover Lisbon for its authenticity of old customs and ancient history, combined with cultural entertainment and hi-tech. It's a city in style, and it should be on your list when visiting the south of Europe. Do not let it escape! The sunshine in Lisbon is present around 290 days a year, and its lowest temperature is about 15°C.

In Lisbon, I recommend you try the salted cod or "bacalhau," which has millions of ways to be cooked. Lisbon is well known for its warm hospitality and its family way of inviting visitors.

Photo Sant George Castle. Lisbon, Portugal

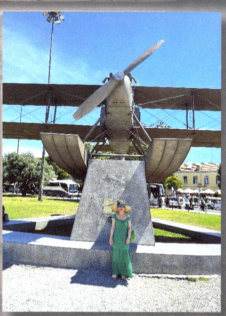

Madeira Island, Portugal

From the moment I arrived, my eyes were delighted with the beautiful sunshine and the beauty of the island of Madeira, whose capital is Funchal.

Discovering Madeira, I realized that the island belongs to the archipelago of islands in Portugal. It's bathed by and seated in the middle of the Atlantic Ocean, and it is like Hawaii, due to its high waves and its unique vegetation of green, thick, and exotic spaces.

At the top of the island, I was enchanted by the beautiful hills, which were occupied by distinct architectural houses and a vast number of banana plantations. The residential areas are very dispersed between the hills, and this is the main reason why the Madeiran way of vehicular transportation is impressive ,with tunnels constructed between the hills giving a great (and the only) way to connect from one hill to the next. Funchal is where the historic center and the port are located, and it is where you will find the most entertainment, bars, restaurants, coffee shops, and stores. These all overlook the boulevard in front of the sea.

On the boulevard, find a relaxing way to finish your day as you enjoy the beautiful sunset.

Speaking of Portugal's gastronomy, it is a mixture of Caribbean, tropical, and Hindu, giving form to its own cuisine.

A market that I had the pleasure to go to was the "Mercado de Lavradores." There, you can sweeten your taste buds, smell the diversity of spices, and delight your retinas with its colorful views and exotic fruits. In this market, you will hear the cacophony of the vendors offering fresh products, while the "senhoras" start conversations with the tourists, giving them a warm welcome, singing, and explaining the best of the traditional Madeiran gastronomy. Fish and fruit are a signature, because Madeira is flooded by its tropical environment, but do not forget to try its variety of meats and typical dessert.

In the antique part of the city, I realized the city's splendor, highlighted with colored houses with their interior squares. It obtained its own personality, full of monumental history combined with bohemian art. This gives the city a perfect modernity and makes it a well-sought destination.

Other places of interest are the cable car, which allows you to get to the top and provides a delightful view and exquisite fresh breeze from the ocean.

They have churches that are combinations of flamenco, hispanic-gothic, and Manuelino styles. Their highlighted roofs—constructed with autochthonous wood—are considered to be some of the most beautiful roofs in Portugal. This makes the churches places of interest to be appreciated.

Madeira is famous for its soccer, and it is the place where patrons and fans of the sport gather to cheer on the Portuguese team. In Madeira was where Rolando, one of the most famous players of the sport, was born.

CHAPTER X

A Trip To Greece (Crete)

Crete is a major island with a very distinct food personality. Its diverse landscapes support farming and herding, millenarian olive trees, and coastal seafood, providing a mind-boggling assortment of edible goods. From these, cooks can create many types of pies: pies filled with kefalograviera cheese (made from sheep and goat milk), orange juice, and cinnamon; pies with wild greens; liver pies; goat cheese pies marinated in orange juice, oregano, and brandy; and sesame cheese tarts.

From the morning's first meal to the evening's soporific finale, Greeks have based their superb cuisine on two native foods: olives and capers.

I noticed that in Greece, meals are divided into three sections: sitos, the grains that make up most of a meal; opson, the main course of meat, fish, vegetables, and sauces; and poton, after-meal drinks and appetizers.

Greece has the most generous mezedes (appetizers) to temper the liquor, and these tasty tidbits are some of the most delightful dishes in Greek cuisine.

Beverages are very important to the Greeks. I found out that in Greece, water is served at every meal—to Greeks, water is osios ("blessed"). Greeks started eating wild grapes and making wine around 11,000 B.C., long before their recorded history! Inhabitants of Constantinople, the ancient capital of the Roman Empire, introduced coffee to Greece, and now the Greeks indulge in it greatly, at home, in coffee shops, or in the squares where they meet to play cards or backgammon. Herbal teas and plant infusions were brought into Greece from China and India to treat illnesses and disorders; even Hippocrates mentioned many hot curatives, especially his famous ptisane (or tisane), a type of barley water. I was surprised to find out that the lemonade we use in America to satiate our summer thirst originated in Greece—the ancient Greeks made syrup from fruit pulp and later added sugar to it, creating fruitades.

Of course, the specialty beverage of Greece is its spicy ouzo, which was developed in the nineteenth century. It's an aperitif distilled from grapes, figs, raisins, and sugars, and flavored with anise.

My trip started at the Leonardo da Vinci-Fiumicino Airport in Rome, where I waited during a three-hour delay. At 8:30 p.m., I finally boarded my easyJet Boeing 727 for a four hour and twenty-minute flight to Heraklion International Airport in Crete, Greece.

Upon my arrival at Heraklion International Airport, I was impressed with the size of the terminal, which resembled a matchbox, with two gates for arrivals and two for departures. It was after midnight, and I was shocked to see everything was closed, including the Avis car rental booth. Only a cafeteria was open, so I bought some coffee to keep me awake. I soon realized I'd be spending the night seated on a bench until Avis opened at 8:00 a.m.

The next morning, I spoke to a surly, unpleasant agent at the car rental booth, and thought to myself that service was better in the U.S. After a while, I got my car—a BMW SUV—that was worth the aggravation. I asked a rental parking lot security guard for directions to my hotel in Makrygyalos. He barely spoke English, but somehow told me to take the Via EO to Irakliou-Agios Nikolaos, then VOEK until E75, and finally merge onto Route E-90. The trip was nearly two hours.

When I reached the resort, I took a hot shower and went to bed. That evening, I got appropriately dressed for a hot, breezy, beautiful night, and I took a tour around the resort. It was crowded, and most of the guests were German and Nordic. There was a welcoming dinner—a banquet-style buffet—along with Greek folk music and dancing.

HISTORY AND LANDMARKS OF CRETE

People have inhabited Crete for over 4,000 years, and you can still vividly feel and taste the history. It has an astounding array of landscapes, colors, and foods to stagger the senses. There are the complex Minoan ruins at Knossos, the ruins at Phaistos, the town of Kato Zakros, the lazy harbor of Agios Nikolaos, the deep Samaria Gorge, the Roman-carved caves on Matala Beach, and the Medieval and Renaissance sites of Rithymo. As I strolled along the sea in Makrygyalos, I was fascinated by the whitewashed houses overlooking the peacock blue sea, and the small taverns and restaurants with tables that almost hugged and kissed the oceanfront, where you can sit and enjoy a typical Greek meal by sunset. On my second night there, my Greek friends invited me to meet them after dinner at one of the wonderful taverns. Here, they joked and talked about the weather, the crops, the theater, and politics, into the wee hours—conversation is very important to them.

Crete has an eclectic character. It's gracious, sometimes austere, authentic, substantial, law-abiding, buzzing with dialogue, and always bold and vital.

This is the land of Zorba, of passionate dances and heartrending dirges.

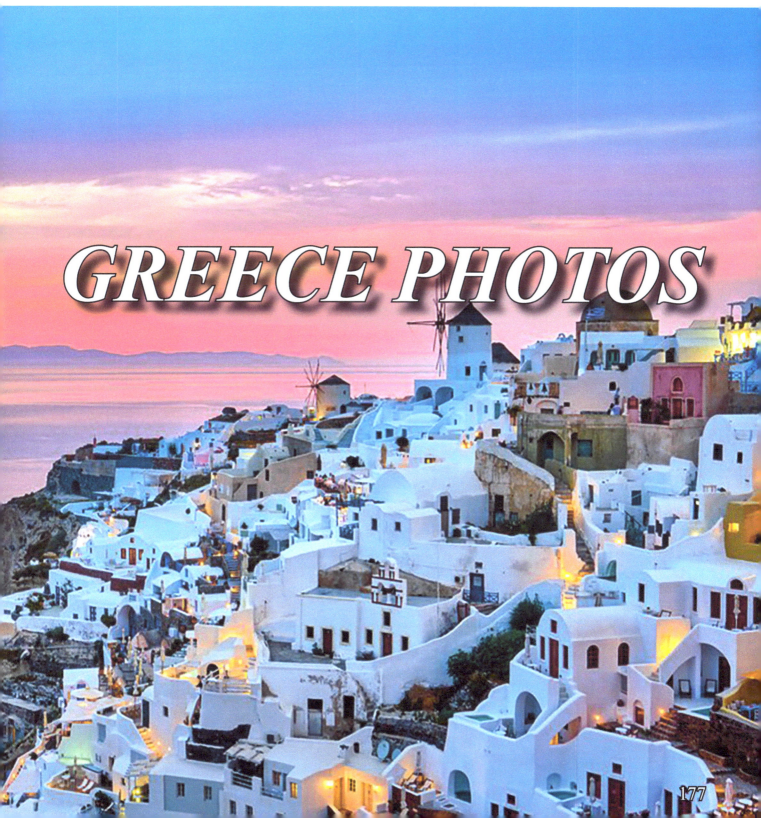

At Hotel Entrance in Crete

Analipsi & Sitia, Lasithi, Greece

Makrygialos, Greece

Heraklion Port, Greece

Aghios Nikolaos Bay, Greece

Greek Appetizers

Spanakopita (Spinach Phyllo Pie)

1 ½ cup spinach
1 cup parsley
1 cup feta cheese
1 pkg. phyllo dough
3 Tbsp. fresh dill, chopped.
8 oz. unsalted butter, melted.
4 egg yolks, beaten
1 Tsp. lemon juice.
Salt and fresh ground black pepper to taste

Directions:

In a bowl, mix spinach, parsley, feta cheese, dill, salt, pepper, eggs, and lemon juice until a paste forms.

Preheat oven to 350°F. In a baking pan greased with melted butter, place half of the package of phyllo dough, one layer at the time, and brush some layers with melted butter. Add spinach mixture to the baking pan and cover with the remaining half of the phyllo dough. Brush some layers with melted butter. Cover the pie completely and bake for about 35 minutes.

Chickpea Rissoles

1 ½ cup chickpeas (soaked overnight covered in water)
7 Tbsp. extra virgin olive oil
2 large onions, chopped.
1 Tbsp. cumin
2 garlic cloves, chopped.
3 Tbsp. flat parsley leaves, chopped.
3-4 fresh sage leaves, chopped.
1 large egg, lightly beaten.
4 Tbsp. self-rising flour
½ cup plain all-purpose flour
Salt and black pepper to taste
Radishes and olives (garnish)

Directions:

Drain chickpeas, rinsing them under cold water until water is clear. In a medium pot, cook chickpeas over a medium-high heat for 1 ¼ -1 ½ hours, or until chickpeas are tender. Set aside some of the liquid from cooking and discard the rest. Put chickpeas in a food processor and add the liquid to produce a velvety mash.

Heat olive oil in a skillet over medium-high heat. Sauté onions, garlic, and sage until brown, then add cumin and parsley. Set aside.

Scrape the chickpea mash into a bowl and add egg, self-rising flour, and sautéed vegetables and herbs. Take a walnut size of the mixture and make a flat hamburger. Cover the rissoles with flour. Heat the remaining oil in a large skillet over high heat and fry rissoles in batches until they are crisp and golden on both sides. Serve hot with radish and olives.

Greek Hummus

14-oz. can chickpeas
4 Tbsp. tahini
2-3 garlic cloves
Juice of ½-1 lemon
Salt and pepper to taste
Whole chickpeas (garnish)

Directions:

Purée chickpeas in the food processor. Add tahini, garlic, lemon juice, salt and pepper. Garnish with chickpeas. Serve at room temperature.

Shrimp-Filled Phyllo Rolls

9-10 sheets phyllo dough, quartered.
(Makes 9" x 7" commercial dough or 7" x 6" inch homemade)
Olive oil or melted butter for oiling phyllo dough.
1 egg yolk, beaten with ½ Tbsp. water.
1 ½ cups béchamel cream
3 Tbsp. Muscat wine
1/3 cup fresh lemon juice
12 oz. raw shrimp shelled & coarsely chopped.
3 Tbsp. chopped fresh dill.
¼ cup chopped fresh chives
Salt to taste

Directions:

Place béchamel cream, salt, wine, lemon juice, shrimps, dill, and chives in a medium-size bowl and stir to mix. Preheat oven to 400°F. Very lightly oil a baking sheet. Brush a rectangle of phyllo lightly with oil. Place about 1 ½ tbsp. of the shrimp mixture in a narrow strip along the side of the rectangle and spread out the full length. Roll the phyllo once over the shrimp, then continue rolling until the filled phyllo is one long roll. Starting on one end of the roll, turn the roll into itself, continuing round and round to make a coil. Place the coil on the prepared baking sheet, seam side down. Lightly oil the top of the roll with oil and brush it with the egg wash (egg yolk beaten with water). Repeat with the remaining phyllo sheets until entire mixture is used. Bake until crisp and golden on top, about 20 minutes. Serve right away at room temperature.

Little Herbed Meatballs

1/2 large onion minced
12 oz of beef or lamb
1/4 cup chopped mint leaves
1 Tsp. fresh chopped oregano or 1/2 teaspoon dried
3/4 Tsp. of salt
1/2 cup finely chopped blanched almonds or
½ coarse bulgur wheat or
1 cup of crushed hazelnuts or Walnuts
1/2 cup of flour
Oil for frying
Fresh mint leaves or parsley leaves for garnish
3 slices of good Greek bread or other crusty bread, crust removed.

1 1/2 Tbsp. of water.
1 1/2 Tbsp. of goat grated cheese.
1/4 cup chopped flat leaf parsley leaves.
1/2 Tbsp. of red wine vinegar
3/4 Tsp. of black pepper

Directions:

Place the onions, water and 1/2 tablespoon of oil in a small saucepan, cover, and bring to a boil over high heat. Reduce the heat and simmer until the water has evaporated, about 5 minutes.

Place the bread in a bowl, add water to cover, and let soak until soft. Remove the bread and squeeze and dry. Mix together with the onion mixture, bread, meat, cheese, chopped herbs, vinegar, salt, and pepper in a large bowl. Cover with plastic wrap, sealing out the air, and refrigerate for 4 hours or up to 2 days.

When ready to cook, roll the meat mixture with your hands into balls the size of a large walnut. Spread the almond or bulgur on one plate and the flour on another. Roll the meatball in the almond or bulgur, then in the flour. Pour oil a depth of 1/2 inch into a large skillet and heat over medium-high heat. Sauté as many meatballs as will fit in one uncrowned until brown all over, about 4 minutes. Transfer them to a towel paper to drain the oil. Repeat. Arrange them on a plate and garnish with mint.

Retsina-Pickled Octopus or Squid

2 small raw octopus, 1 ½ lbs. each, pounded and cleaned OR
1 ½ lbs. raw squid steaks OR
1 ½ lbs. cooked octopus or squid steaks

Simmering liquid:
¾ cup water
2 Tbsp. olive oil
¾ cup white wine vinegar

Pickling solution:
½ cup Retsina wine
2 garlic cloves, chopped
1 small bay leaf, crushed.
1 Tsp. fresh fennel frond, chopped.
½ Tsp. mustard seeds
¼ Tsp. salt
1/8 Tsp. fresh ground black pepper
Parsley sprigs, olives, and capers for garnish

Directions:

If using raw octopus or squid steaks, place them in a large pot. Add the ingredients for simmering liquid and bring to a boil. Reduce heat and simmer, covered, until tender, 45 minutes to 1 hour for octopus or 2-3 minutes for squid steaks. Drain in a colander, keeping the liquid, and set aside until cool enough to handle.

If using cooked octopus or squid steaks, cut octopus into ¼-inch thick slices. Cut squid steaks into 1-inch wide strips. Place in a bowl or dish that is large enough to hold the reserve liquid. In a medium-size pot, combine the reserve liquid and ingredients for the pickling solution and bring to a boil. Let boil 1 minute, then pour over octopus or squid. Cover and chill overnight or as long as 3 days. To serve, transfer the octopus to a platter or individual plates and garnish with parsley, olives, and capers.

Greek Side Dishes

Greek Olive Bread

2 red onions
2 Tbsp. extra virgin olive oil
2 cups pitted black or green olives.
7 cups white bread flour (high in gluten)
1 ½ Tbsp. salt
4 Tbsp. rapid rise yeast
3 Tbsp. flat leaf parsley leaves, chopped.
Pinch of sugar
2 cups water

Directions:

Heat olive oil in a skillet over medium-high heat and sauté onions until light brown. Add olives.

In warm water, add yeast with a pinch of sugar and let it rise for about 10 minutes. Mix yeast with flour, salt, parsley, and sautéed onions and olives. Add more water if the dough feels dry. Put dough on a lightly floured surface and knead for 10 minutes. Cover dough with a kitchen towel and leave it in a warm room to rise and double in bulk.

Preheat oven to 425°F. Lightly grease two baking sheets. Slash the tops of the loaves with a knife. Bake for about 40 minutes or until golden brown. When tapped on the bottom, it should sound hollow. Transfer to cool on a rack. Serve with Greek butter or Greek salad.

Braised Artichokes with Fresh Peas

4 medium-large artichokes
Juice of 2 lemons
2/3 cup extra virgin olive oil.
1 onion thinly sliced.
4-5 spring onions (scallions)
2 carrots, peeled & shredded.
2 ½ lbs. fresh peas
1 cup hot water
2/3 cup dry white wine
4 Tbsp. fresh dill, chopped.
Salt and pepper to taste
Sprig of fresh dill (garnish)

Directions:

Remove and discard outer leaves of artichokes. Cut off tops and cut artichokes lengthwise. Scoop the hairy part. Drop pieces in a bowl of water with lemon juice.

Heat oil in a medium skillet. Sauté spring onions until brown, then add carrots and sauté for about 5 minutes. Add peas and stir for about 2 minutes.

Place artichokes in a pot of boiling water with more lemon juice. Cover and cook for about 45 minutes, stirring occasionally. Add dill and cook for a few more minutes.

Place artichokes and vegetables in a baking dish. Add wine, taste seasoning, and bake for 15-20 minutes. Serve hot. Garnish with chopped dill.

Greek Potato Zucchini Casserole

½ cup extra virgin olive oil
1 large onion
3 garlic cloves, crushed.
4 large, ripe tomatoes peeled and chopped.
2 ¼ lbs. small red potatoes, cut into wedges.
2 zucchinis, sliced.
¼-inch thick
Salt and pepper to taste
Fresh parsley leaves (garnish)

Directions:

Preheat oven to 350°F. Coat potatoes with olive oil and place in a baking dish. Heat the oil in a medium skillet over medium-high heat and sauté onion and garlic until brown. Add tomatoes, season, and cook for about 5 minutes.

Mix potatoes and zucchini with the sautéed vegetables. Place on medium oven shelf and cook for 30 minutes or until potatoes are tender. Garnish with chopped parsley leaves on top. Serve hot.

Greek Tomato and Potato Bake

½ cup extra virgin olive oil
1 large onion
3 garlic cloves, crushed.
4 large, ripe tomatoes peeled and chopped.
2 ¼ lbs. small red potatoes, cut into wedges.
2 zucchinis, sliced.
¼-inch thick
Salt and pepper to taste
Fresh parsley leaves (garnish)

Directions:

Preheat oven to 350F. Coat potatoes with olive oil and place in a baking dish. Heat oil in a medium skillet over medium-high heat, and sauté onion and garlic until brown. Add tomatoes, season, and cook for about 5 minutes.

Mix potatoes with the sautéed vegetables. Place on medium oven shelf and cook for 45 minutes or until potatoes are tender. Garnish with chopped parsley leaves on top. Serve hot.

Russian Salad

4 oz. fresh green beans, trimmed & diced into ¼" cubes
1 medium carrot, trimmed & diced into ¼" cubes
1 medium red or white potato, peeled & diced into ¼" cubes
½ Tbsp. capers, minced
1 large hardboiled egg, chopped
1 medium Granny Smith apple, peeled & chopped
½ cup fresh shelled peas.
½ cup fresh baby lima beans.
½ cup lemony mayonnaise.
½ Tbsp. salt
¼ cup dill, chopped.
¼ cup pickles

Directions:

Bring a medium pot of water to a boil over high heat and cook peas until tender. Return to boil and cook the carrot until barely tender, about 3 minutes. Return to boil and cook lima beans for about 5 minutes. Return to boil and cook potato until barely tender or until it holds its shape, about 6 minutes.

When ready to dress the salad, whisk together mayonnaise, salt, capers, pickles, and dill in a bowl. Toss the vegetables, apple, and eggs together and stir in half of mayonnaise mixture. Transfer salad to a serving plate and spread the remaining mayonnaise mixture over the top to cover completely, like a frosting. Store in refrigerator until chilled.

Greek Dessert

Baklava

¾ cup butter, melted
14 oz. pkg. phyllo pastry dough sheets
2 Tbsp. lemon juice
4 Tbsp. honey
¼ cup superfine sugar
Zest of 1 lemon
2 Tbsp. cinnamon
1 ¾ cup blanched almonds, chopped.
1 ¾ cup walnuts, chopped.
¾ cup pistachios, chopped

Syrup:
1 ¾ cup superfine sugar
½ cup honey
2 ½ cups water
2 strips lemon rind

Directions:

Place 1 pastry dough sheet in the tin and brush with a little melted butter. Repeat the procedure until using half of the pastry dough sheets. Cover with paper towel and set aside.

Filling: Place lemon juice, honey, and sugar in a pan and heat gently, stirring continuously until completely dissolved. Stir in lemon rinds, cinnamon, and nuts.

Spread half the filling evenly over pastry dough sheets and cover with three layers of sheets, brushing butter on each layer as you go and spreading the remaining filling over the pastry. Finish with the remaining sheets, always brushing them with butter as you go. Use a sharp knife to mark the pastry into squares, almost cutting through the filling. Bake until crispy or golden brown.

Meanwhile, prepare the syrup. Place sugar, honey, water, and lemon rinds in a medium saucepan on low heat, and stir until sugar and honey dissolve. Bring to a boil until the mixture has slightly thickened, about 10 minutes. Remove syrup from heat and let cool slightly.

Remove baklava from oven. Remove lemon rinds from syrup, then pour syrup over the baklava. Leave to soak overnight. Cut into squares, decorate with chopped pistachios, and serve.

Date & Almond Tart

1 ½ cup all-purpose flour
6 Tbsp. butter
1 egg

Filling:
7 Tbsp. butter
1 cup superfine sugar
1 egg beaten.
1 cup ground almond flour
2 Tbsp. all-purpose flour
2 Tbsp. orange flower water
12-13 dates, halved & pitted.
4 Tbsp. apricot jam

Directions:

Preheat oven to 400°F. Place a baking sheet in the oven. Sift all-purpose flour into a bowl, add butter, and work with fingertips until mixture resembles fine breadcrumbs.

Add egg and 1 tbsp. cold water, then work to a smooth dough. Roll out the pastry dough on a slightly floured surface and line the dough into an 8-inch tart pan. Prick the base with fork, then chill until needed.

Filling: Cream the butter and sugar until a light cream, then beat egg. Stir almond flour, all-purpose flour, and 1 tbsp. orange flower water. Spread the mixture into the pastry dough. Arrange the dates cut side down.

Bake on a hot baking sheet for 10-15 minutes, then reduce heat to 350°F for another 15-20 minutes or until golden brown. Transfer tart to a rack to cool. Gently heat the apricot jam and mix with the remaining orange flower water. Brush tart with the jam and serve room temperature.

CHAPTER XI

Back on the Train to Buffalo

The young, handsome man and I continued talking nonstop. He asked me for my nationality, which he could not figure out from my accent. I smiled and answered proudly that I was originally a Venezuelan Jewish girl. I explained to him that perhaps the fact that I'm a polyglot had affected my original native accent.

After recounting all these amazing trips throughout Southern Europe, which has been part of my culinary journey, I could tell that he was very tired. I spoke so much, to the point that I think I became intolerable. So, he put his earphones on and acted as if I had become invisible. I did feel that I did not want to stop, and I hoped somebody had simply phoned him so we could continue our conversation. The trip to Buffalo by train can be long and tedious, just like a snake's fart, and I needed distraction.

Suddenly, he received a phone call, and by his conversation, I realized he was talking with his wife. He informed her that he would get off at the next stop and would be home for dinner.

After he hung up, I told him that I had made a couple of wraps with kosher smoked turkey, tomatoes, and lettuce with a homemade Dijon mayo dressing that I learned when I was studying in France. I offered him some with homemade brownies that I was bringing to Buffalo for Lily.

He ate them and was very impressed. He said the food was superb, but he could not share it with his wife, because she was not a good cook.

He started to put his things together, closing his computer. He got up and grabbed his mini suitcase, and with a smile in his face, he told me that maybe he would see me on one of the cooking shows. He wished me good luck with my future endeavors. Then he walked away through the train aisle and disappeared.

I closed my eyes and fell asleep until I heard the train conductor announcing that the following stop was Buffalo, so I took my mini suitcase from the upper compartment and walked down the aisle to the door, waiting for it to open.

In the Buffalo station, I saw my son in the distance. I walked to the car, and after a big hug and kiss, he directed me to where Lily was. Then, after seeing her, I was sure that there could be no greater beauty and perfection from G-d. She was totally a world of joy.

My trip to Buffalo could not be more worthy than any of the great delicatessens!

Printed in the USA
CPSIA information can be obtained
at www.ICGtesting.com
LVHW062053020224
770831LV00036B/366